LAST MAN

3

The Chase

Balak + Sanlaville + Vivès

First Second
New York

ONI, STOP IT!
GRRR!
THEY'RE *MY* DATES!
YOU'VE EATEN ALREADY!
WRUM!
STOP!
MOM!
RUFF!
ONI!
ADRIAN!
GRRR.

I NEED SOME PEACE AND QUIET, PLEASE.
SEE?
YOU'RE A PAIN.
GRRR.
THIS DAMN MAP! IF ONLY...OKAY, THINK...IF MY HUNCH IS RIGHT, HE HEADED EAST.
STRAIGHT TOWARD THE RIFT.

MOM?
DO YOU KNOW WHERE RICHARD WENT?
ARE YOU DONE EATING?
YEAH.
WANT ME TO SHOW YOU HOW THE BIKE WORKS?
OH-
YEAH!
THAT'S THE MOTOR, WHICH DRIVES THE CHAIN THAT MOVES THE WHEEL.
USING THE SPIRIT OF THE WIND?
NO, SOMETHING ELSE.

THE BIKE HAS A CONTAINER CALLED THE TANK, WHERE YOU ADD A LIQUID...
THAT LIQUID IS WHAT POWERS THE BIKE.
"GASOLINE."
HERE, HOLD THE CAP.
IT STINKS!
HEH HEH.
OKAY, GRAB YOUR STUFF. WE STILL HAVE A WAYS TO GO.
MOM?

WHY WAS THE BIKE IN THE BASEMENT?

A MAN LEFT IT FOR ME.
AND THE MAP TOO?
YES, ALONG WITH THE HELMET AND GLOVES.

HE GAVE YOU EVERYTHING?
KIND OF.

EEEP!!!
ONI!
WHAT'S GOING ON?
GRRR.
MOM!
ONI'S NOT FEELING WELL.
MRRRR..R
TAP

RAWR!
ONI! QUIET!
RAWR!
WE'RE HERE.

THE RIFT!
RAWR RAWR...

HISSS!

ONI!
RAWR!

NO!
LEAVE HIM, ADRIAN.

HE'S BETTER OFF IN THE VALLEY OF KINGS.

MOM, I'VE GOT SAND IN MY EYES.
MOVE AWAY FROM THE EDGE, SWEETIE, TO STAY OUT OF THE WIND.
MMM...
DO YOU REMEMBER THE SONG "THE BREATH OF THE IGUANA QUEEN"?
"FORSWEAR ALL PROFANE DEEDS, SEEN OR UNSEEN, FOR NAUGHT ESCAPES THE BREATH OF THE IGUANA QUEEN."
"EARTH, HEAVENS, HER BREATH FEEDS ALL..."
"...FROM THE LARGEST OF THE LARGE TO THE SMALLEST OF THE SMALL."
"WITHIN HER BOSOM REIGNS LIFE'S POWER; BEYOND LIES A COLD NIGHT OF TERROR..."
"PITY THOSE WHO STRAY TOO FAR AFIELD..."
"...FROM THE IGUANA QUEEN'S WARM SHIELD..."
WELL, A LONG TIME AGO, PEOPLE WROTE THAT SONG ABOUT THIS PLACE.

THE BREATH OF THE IGUANA QUEEN...THEY CALL IT THE ETHEREAL SOURCE IN CHURCH. IT'S THE SOURCE OF LIFE, AND THE POWER YOU DRAW FROM WHEN YOU SUMMON THE SPIRITS.
OH...

YES, MASTER JANSEN TOLD US ABOUT IT. BUT ELORNA SAYS THE BREATH IS THE SOULS OF FIGHTERS WHO DIED. ISN'T THAT WEIRD?
THE TWO MIGHT NOT BE MUTUALLY EXCLUSIVE.

LISTEN, ADRIAN, THEY SAY A LOT OF THINGS IN SCHOOL AND AT CHURCH, BUT IN THE END...

...WHAT SHOULD YOU ALWAYS LISTEN TO?

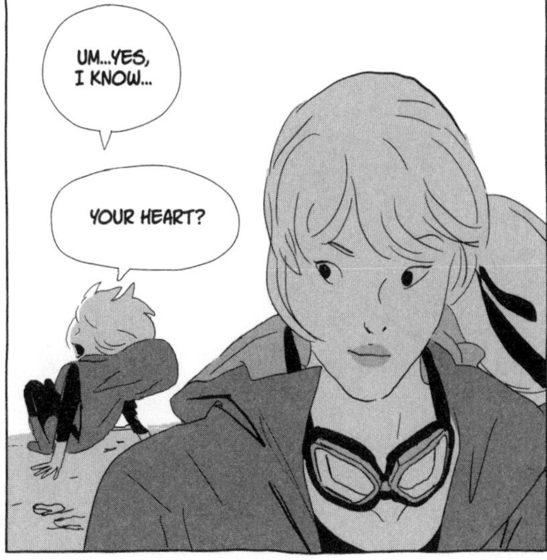
UM...YES, I KNOW...
YOUR HEART?

NO, SILLY!
WHAT YOUR MOTHER SAYS.
AND I KNOW THAT THE RIFT IS FAR MORE THAN ALL THAT.
ADRIAN, COME AND SEE.
MOTORCYCLE TRACKS. MY HUNCH WAS RIGHT.
I DON'T GET IT. ANOTHER MOTORCYCLE?
ALDANA... WE'RE REALLY GONNA HAVE TO TALK.

ADRIAN...
GIVE ME YOUR HAND.
I'M GOING TO SCOUT THE WAY AHEAD. I'LL BE GONE FIVE MINUTES.
PROMISE TO STAY PUT. OKAY?
OKAY... BUT YOU'RE GOIN' IN *THERE?*
YES. BUT I'LL BE BACK SHORTLY.

MOM'S TAKING A WALK INTO THE BREATH OF THE IGUANA QUEEN.

RRRRRRRRRRRRRRr
ADRIAN!
DON'T MOVE-
I'LL BE RIGHT
BACK!

WOOSH

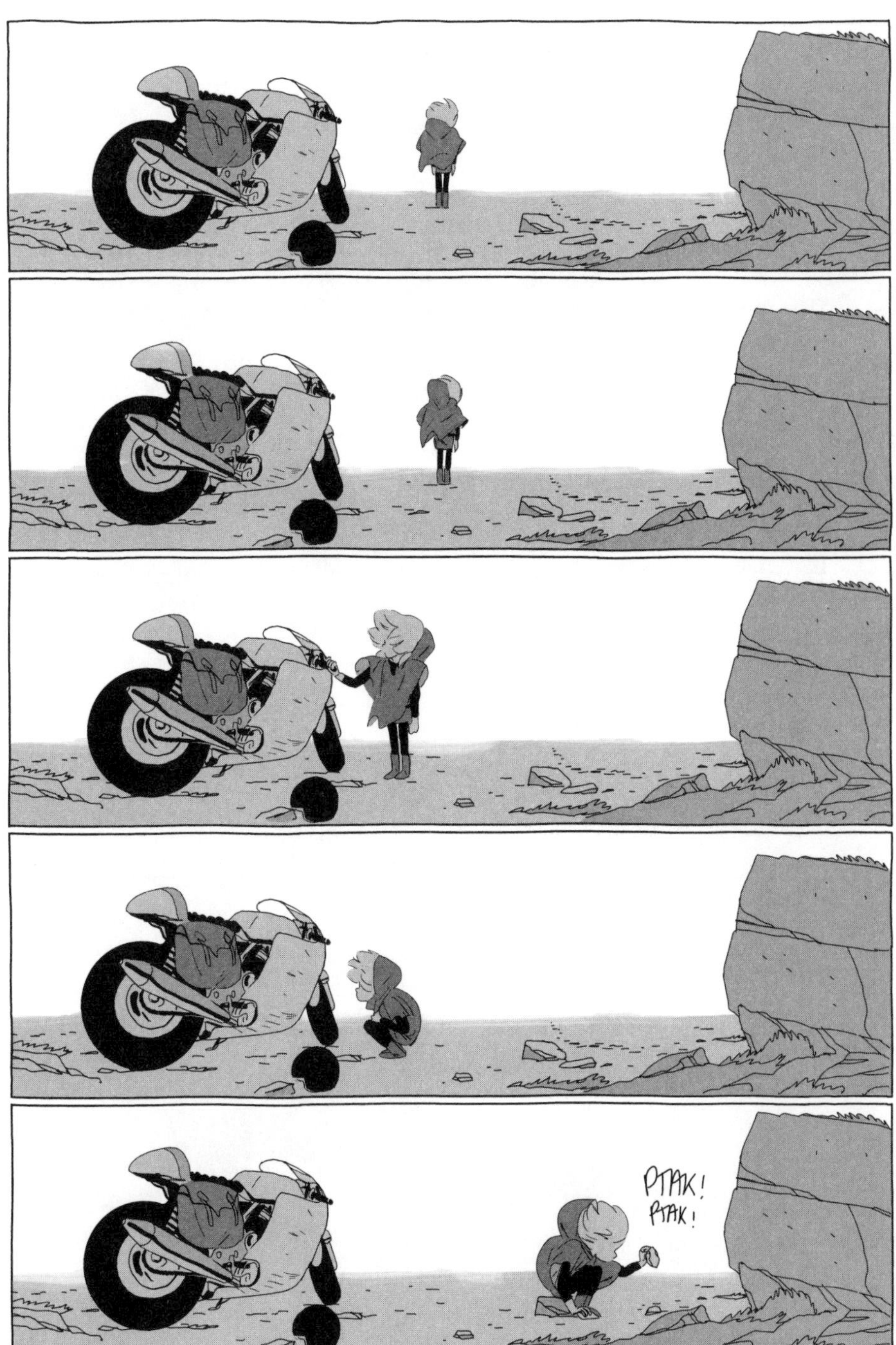
PTAK!
PTAK!

CRRR
SHKRRR
FRROUSHH

RRRRRRR RRRRRRRRRRRR

MOM?

TAP!

I DON'T KNOW IF THE RIFT IS WHERE THE SOULS OF FIGHTERS COME TO REST OR IF IT REALLY IS THE "ETHEREAL SOURCE"...
...BUT THERE ARE TWO THINGS I DO KNOW, ADRIAN: THE RIFT'S A BORDER...
...AND ALSO A CROSSING POINT. AND ON THE OTHER SIDE, SOMEONE ELSE KNOWS IT TOO.
SOMEONE WHO USED THIS MAP TO COME HERE.

NOTE REGARDING THE RIFT: TAKE THE RIDGE BETWEEN THE TWO VALLEYS...
THE PEAKS JOIN UP TO FORM A PLATEAU...
IT'S PASSABLE...

KEEP GOING STRAIGHT AHEAD.
MROOOOOoo
CLACVROOOOOO
THE PATH'S CLEAR...

CROSSING IS EASY, DESPITE THE THICK FOG AND SIDE WINDS.
VROOOOM
IF THE LEGEND IS TRUE, AND THE MAP'S CORRECT...
CLACK!

RRRRVRRRROOA
ARRRVRRRBROOO
...I SHOULD BE ARRIVING AT THE VALLEY OF KINGS.
OOO

!!!
RRDO
SCREE!

WE'RE ALMOST THERE. IT'S GONNA GET BUMPY.
MMM...
HOLD ON TIGHT!
WWROOOOOOAAAR
TOC!
VROOAAAR CLACK BROOOAAAR

BROOOOOOoo
ROOOBR
OOO
PRROO
CLACC

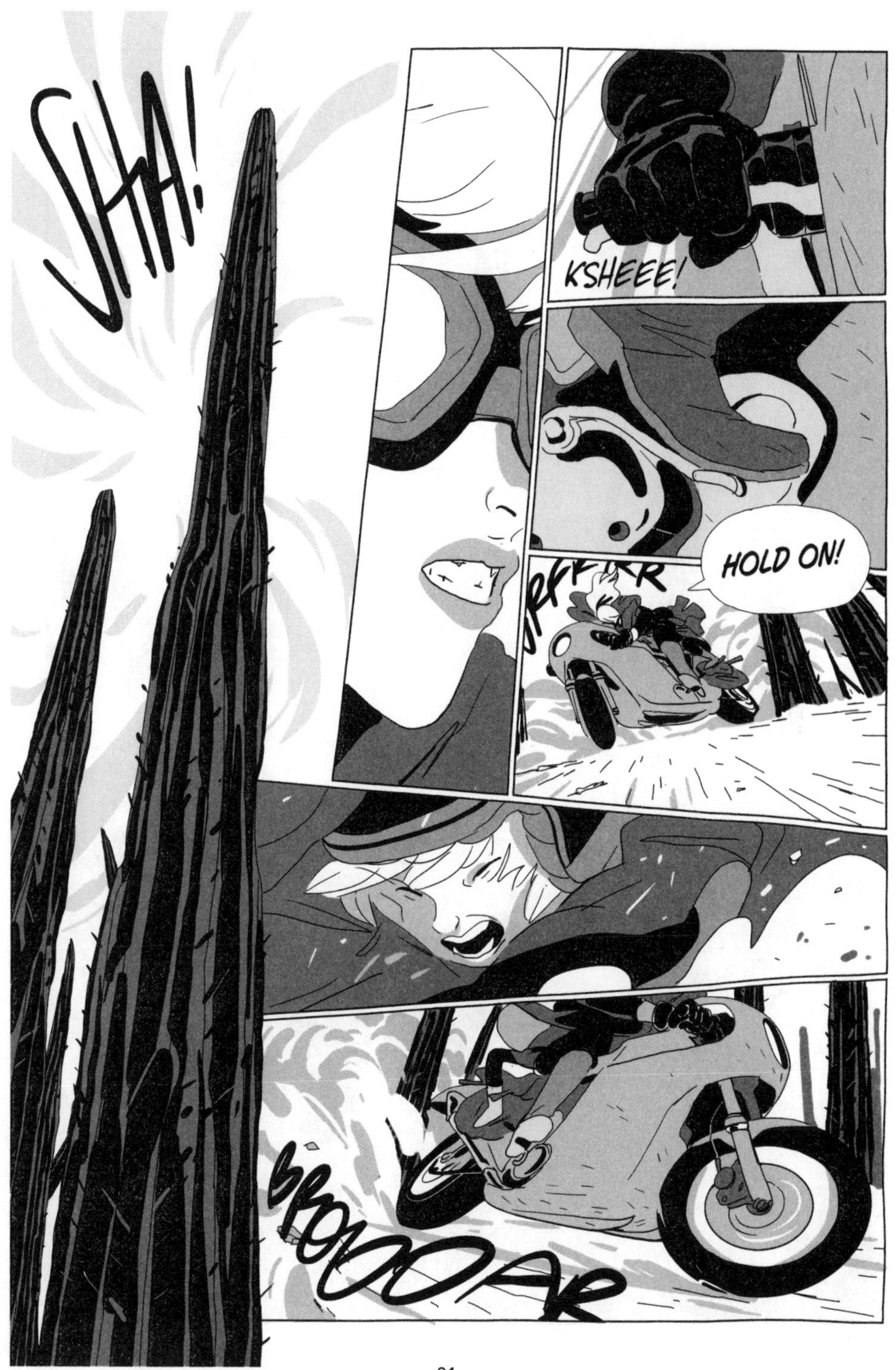
SHA!
KSHEEE!
HOLD ON!
BROOOAR

HA!
WHAT THE...

WHAT KIND OF TREES ARE THESE?

PLOP
PLOP

SHOOT, WE'RE ALREADY DOWN TO THE FUEL RESERVE.

WE'RE GONNA HAVE TO CONSERVE GAS. LET'S WALK A BIT.

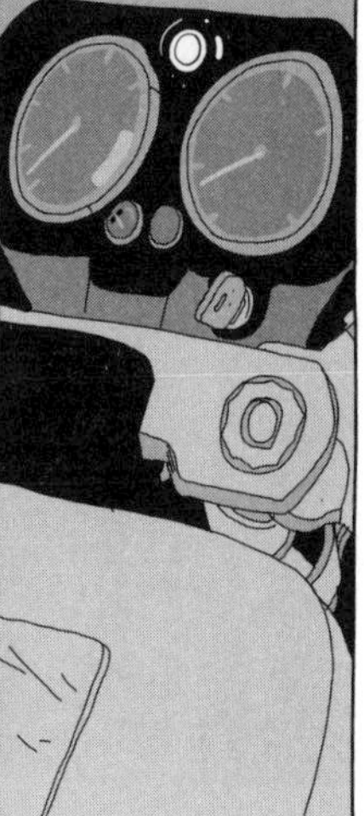

DID YOU DRINK SOME WATER, ADRIAN?
YEAH.

HOW ARE WE GONNA FIND GASOLINE?
THEY HAVE IT EVERYWHERE OVER HERE. YOU CAN BUY IT.

WITH GOLD COINS?
AMONG OTHER THINGS.

WHAT'S THAT?
IT'S KIND OF LIKE A BIKE WITH FOUR WHEELS.
WHOSE IS IT?
NOBODY'S—IT'S ABANDONED.
IT'S CALLED A CAR.
NO FUEL, OF COURSE.
WHY DIDN'T WE EVER USE THE BIKE IN THE VALLEY OF KINGS?
MOM?
BECAUSE WE MANAGED JUST FINE WITHOUT IT.
MMM.

CAW
CAW
CAW
CAW CAW
LOOK, ADRIAN.
CAW
CAW
ADRI...
CAW
CAW

ADRIAN...
ADRIAN, LOOK.
LOOK HOW PRETTY IT IS ON ME.
I ALWAYS HOLD THIS CLOSE TO MY HEART.
JUST AS CLOSE AS I HOLD THOUGHTS ABOUT YOU.
ELORNA!
I'M A WOMAN NOW, ADRIAN.

YOU KNOW WHO GAVE ME THIS RING?
MY HUSBAND.
RICH-

HAVE SOME WATER, ADRIAN. IT'S GETTING HOT.

HEY, LOOK!

I KNEW IT WAS THIS WAY!

YOU KNEW A VILLAGE WAS HERE?
WHY IS IT DESERTED?
IT'S NOT A VILLAGE, IT'S A STATION.
ADRI–
ADRIAN, WHAT ARE YOU DOING?
MOM, CHECK IT OUT, A BIKE!

LOOK, IT'S ABANDONED...
I'M NOT SURE IT'S ABANDONED.
YOU THINK IT'S RICHARD'S?
I DON'T THINK SO...
NOT HIS STYLE.
THE TANK IS ALMOST FULL.
KLONG!
KLONG!
LET'S SIPHON THE GAS.
WE'LL NEED A HOSE.
BRING OVER THAT JERRICAN, SWEETIE.
THE WHAT?
THE CAN, OVER THERE.
YOU GOT IT?
YEAH.
HURRY UP, SWEETIE.

AM I HOLDING IT RIGHT?
YUCK!
IT'S REALLY NASTY!
YOU SWALLOWED SOME?
UGH! GASOLINE TASTES DISGUSTING!
BUT WITH THAT WE CAN LEAVE.
VRRRR!!!
VRRRR...

I KNEW IT.

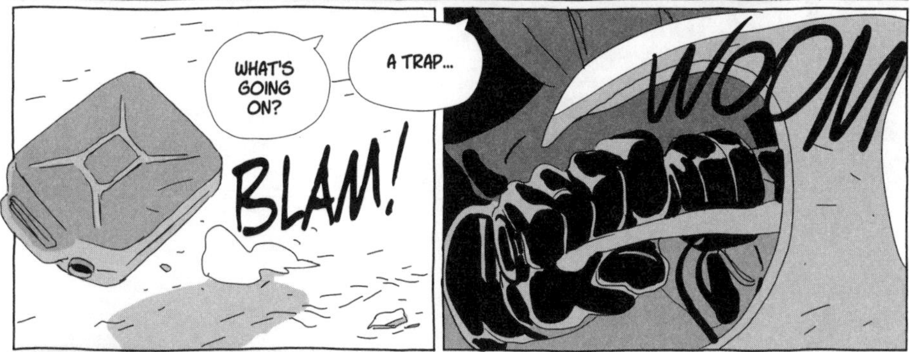
WHAT'S GOING ON?
A TRAP...
BLAM!
WOOM

VRAAA AR VRAAAAA
WAAAARRR

VROOOOOM

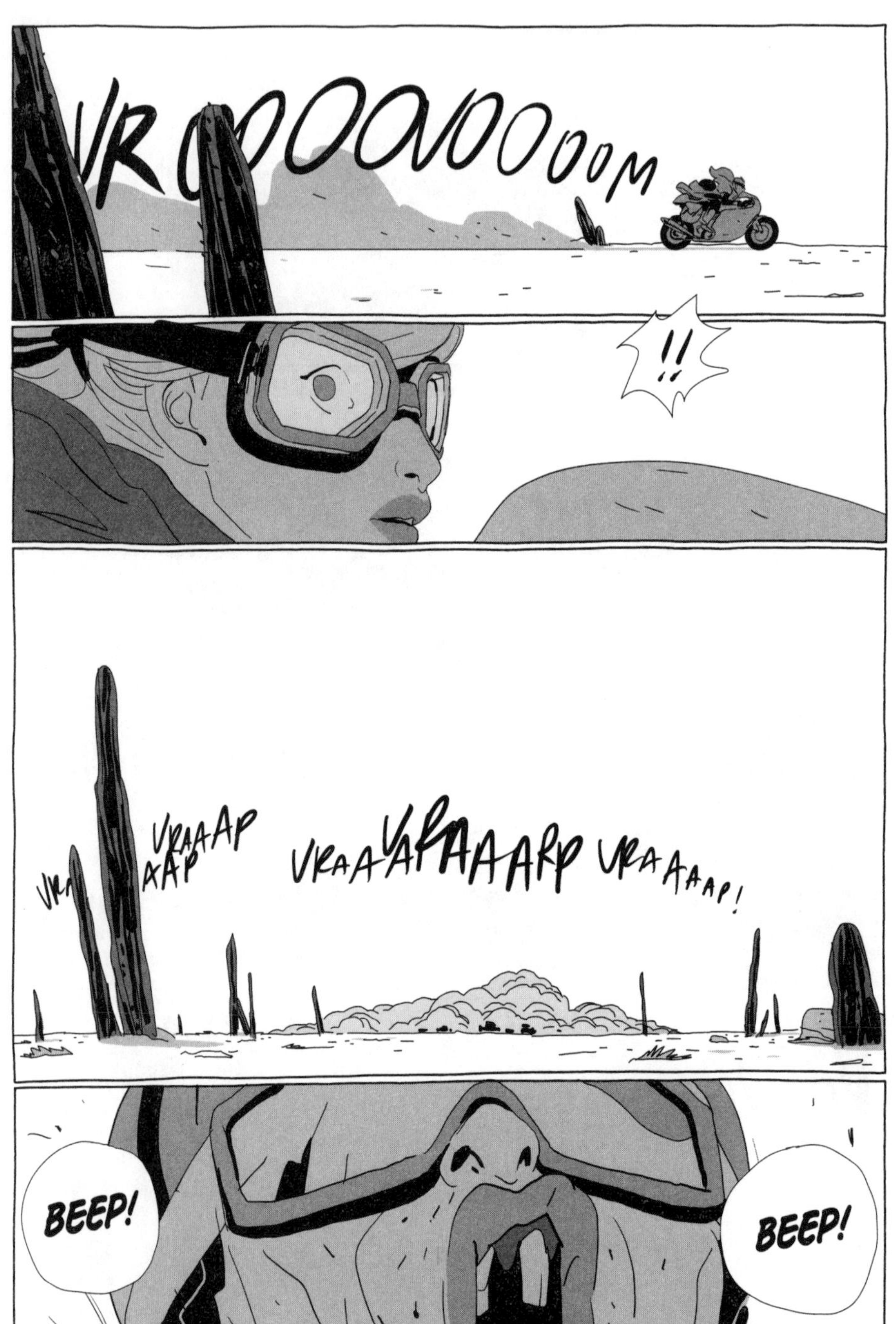
VROOOOOOOOOOM
!!
VRAAAP
VRAAAP
VRAAAAAARP
VRAAAAAP!
BEEP!
BEEP!

VRAAAAP
VRAAAAOPVRAAAA
RRRSHKRRRRK
SHVRAAAA
VRO
WOOOM
VROOM
VRA
HEEEY!
HI HI!
WOM
HO
VRA
AAP
BEEP-BEEP!
HAHA
HA!
VRA

YA THINK YOU'RE AT GRANNY'S, HOODLUMS? LEVEL 1 TERRITORIAL INVASION AND AGGRAVATED ROBBERY!
NOTHING ESCAPES THE WATCHFUL EYE OF THE NILLIPOLIS TURBOPOLICE FORCE! THE UNSTOPPABLE HAMMER OF JUSTICE IS ABOUT TO FALL!
LOOKS LIKE WE TOOK THE BAIT...
BEEP-BEEP!
KINDLY PRESENT ME YOUR LICENSE, OR IT'S GONNA GET UGLY.

WE'RE NOT FROM AROUND HERE...
WE AREN'T USED TO DEALING WITH THUGS.
THUGS? INSULTING A GOVERNMENT AGENT AS HE CARRIES OUT HIS HONORABLE DUTIES! YOU'RE MAKING MATTERS WORSE FOR YOURSELF!
OKAY, BOYS, WE DON'T HAVE ALL DAY.
SARGEANT! IDENTIFY THE VEHICLE TYPE AND PUT THAT CRAP IN THE FILE.
LOOKS LIKE WE'VE GOT A TWO-WHEEL-DRIVE MOTORCYCLE, MODEL NUMBER 1211-VMAXMIC.

VERY GOOD.
WE CAN NOW PROCEED WITH THE RAPE OF THE DELINQUENT.
WHAT'S A RAPE?
LISTEN, WE'VE ONLY GOT A SMALL BIT OF MONEY AND SOME FOOD....
WE'LL GIVE ALL OF IT TO YOU.
BUT LEAVE US THE MOTORCYCLE– WE NEED IT.

BEEP-BEEP!
HANG ON A SEC, KIDDIES...PULL YOUR PANTS BACK UP.
I HEREBY DEMAND TO INSPECT THE HOOLIGANS' EVIDENCE.
AW C'MON, BOSS!
PFFF... OKAY, BOSS...
THE DATES ARE TASTY...
SO, WHAT'VE WE GOT HERE? DATES-BAH! WATER...WHO CARES? AH! GOLD COINS!
WE'RE DEFINITELY CONFISCATING THIS!
THE MOTORCYCLE TOO, WHICH IS OBVIOUSLY STOLEN!

HEY, CUTIE PIE, THAT HELMET OF YOURS SURE LOOKS NICE!
I BET IT'LL LOOK GOOD ON MY HEAD TOO!
OWWW!
SHTAK!
HEY!

YOU LAY ONE HAND ON MY SON, YOU'LL REGRET YOU WERE BORN.
PFF HA HA
HA HA HA!

HA HA!
HA HA!
HA HA!
HA!
HA HA HA!
HEE
HEE HEE!
OKAY, SORRY.
HERE, YOU CAN HAVE YOUR HELMET...
...DAMN BRAT!
SLAP!
...

HA
HA!
HA
HA HA!
AH,
KIDS...
THEY'RE A
RIOT!
HUH?
...SPIRITS,
POWERS
BEYOND
THE
HEAVENS...
LIGHTNING,
THUNDER,
SHIELD
OF THE
GUARDIANS...
SPIRIT
OF THE
WIND...
PUNISH!

WH...
WHA...
WHAT WAS...
...

GNNN...

MOM...
HOW... HOW'D YOU DO THAT?

THAT WAS THE SCHOOL-OF-HEAVENS SUMMONING...

MOM!
YOU CAN DO THE SCHOOL-OF-HEAVENS SUMMONG?!

LET'S TALK ABOUT IT LATER, OKAY?

THAT OUGHTTA DO IT...

HEY, IT'S MAKING NOISE...
WHAT IS THIS?

SOMETHING FOR TALKING BETWEEN LONG DISTANCES. PUT IT BACK. WE DON'T TAKE THINGS THAT AREN'T OURS.

WE AREN'T BANDITS...
...WHO HELP THEMSELVES TO OTHER PEOPLE'S THINGS.

OKAY?

OKAY.

BUT THE GASOLINE'S OKAY?
HMM...
YES, WE'RE JUST BORROWING IT FOR THE TRIP.
HUFF...
HUFF...
HA...
HAA...
HUH...
WHAT WAS... WHAT WAS THAT... THAT... WOMAN?
SHE'S BAD...
...NEWS.
SKREEK

THIS IS BUGGY PATROL!
BUGGY PATROL, CODE RED!
HAH!
HUH HUH...
BUGGY PATROL, THIS IS TRUCK PATROL!
TRUCK PATROL, WE'VE GOT A CODE RED...
A BIG ONE!
CODE RED? WHAT THE HELL IS THIS CRAP? OVER.
YOU REMEMBER THAT GUY WE NABBED YESTERDAY, THAT THE BOSS LET GO?
YEAH.
WELL, WE FOUND A GIRL IN THE SAME SPOT.
AND YOU'RE CALLING A CODE RED FOR *THAT?!* OVER.
I'M CALLING A CODE RED BECAUSE...

VROOOOOM!
SHHH
SHHH
VRRR
BUGGY PATROL, I DIDN'T HEAR THE END OF YOUR SENTENCE. OVER...
WELL, YOU'RE ABOUT TO RUN INTO HER...

WATCH OUT, SHE KICKED OUR...
HEY, GUYS! THEY'RE SENDING US A CHICK...
HA
HA!
SHE BETTER BE HOT!
VRRR
...
BLAM!
VRRR
THAT WAS THE CHICK?
SHE SEEMED REALLY HOT.

VRRRR...

ADRIAN...
DO YOU SMELL THAT?

THE SALT IN THE AIR...?

THAT'LL BE 60 BUCKS FOR PARKING...
...AND 120 FOR THEFT INSURANCE, VALID FOR TWO HOURS.
THEFT INSURANCE?
YEAH. THESE ARE HARD TIMES!
HERE— WILL THIS DO?
WHAT IS IT WITH THESE COINS? YOU GUYS ARE A PAIN!
EXCUSE ME, BUT DID SOMEONE ELSE USE THAT CURRENCY?
HMM? YES, YESTERDAY— A GUY, KINDA HOT.
HE STILL IN TOWN?
GO SEE FOR YOURSELF! ***NEXT!***
ELEVATOR FOR DOWNTOWN NILLIPOLIS! 3 SECONDS!
HURRY UP, ADRIAN. RICHARD'S HERE—I JUST KNOW IT!

KLANG

REMEMBER THAT BIG BODY OF WATER WE SAW? WELL, IT'S GOT LOTS OF BOATS...AND THOSE BOATS COME HERE.
THEY CALL THIS A PORT. TONS OF PEOPLE PASS THROUGH.
CINEMA
STAY CLOSE. THESE AREN'T LIKE PEOPLE FROM THE VALLEY.
WE HAVE TO BE REALLY CAREF–
AAAARGH

I'M NEVER SETTING FOOT IN THIS DUMP AGAIN!
THAT'S RIGHT—BEAT IT!
AND DON'T COME BACK!
SHOW
GIRLS
FAT CHANCE! WITH SERVICE LIKE THAT, YOU'LL BE OUTTA BUSINESS IN NO TIME, SKANK!
HA HA! THANKS FOR THE ADVICE, JACKASS!
FLORA! RELAX!
I *AM* RELAXED!
C'MON, ADRIAN...
?

LOSER!
COME ON, CHILL OUT!
IT'S NO BIG DEAL!
NO BIG DEAL? THAT CREEP WAS TAKING OUT HIS ANGER ON ME!
THE WORST PART IS, HE'S RIGHT. I'D SHUT THIS PLACE DOWN!
SHOW
HALF THE GIRLS HAVE LEFT, SO YOU'D BETTER START MOVING YOUR ASS, AND WIPE THAT GRIN OFF...

HEY, MISS!
CINEMA
YOU'RE REALLY BEAUTIFUL... AND IF YOU'RE LOOKING FOR WORK...
...WELL, YOU'RE IN LUCK, BECAUSE YOU'RE HIRED!
HOW 'BOUT IT?
NO, THANKS.
BUT YOU CAN TELL ME WHERE TO FIND THE BEST BARS.
BARS, HUH? SO YOU'RE LOOKING FOR A GOOD TIME? COME CHECK OUT OUR PLACE.

WE AREN'T HERE FOR A GOOD TIME!
SORRY!
WAIT!
WHAT ABOUT A HOTEL? IF YOU NEED ONE, I HAVE FREE ROOMS.
UP TO THE END OF YOUR STAY.
REALLY?
I HOPE YOU DIDN'T PAY FOR THE PARKING LOT'S THEFT INSURANCE, AT LEAST?

IT'S VERY KIND OF YOU. IF WE NEED SOMETHING, WE'LL BE BACK.
THANKS!
ARE YOU HUNGRY AT ALL, ADRIAN? I THINK WE SHOULD FIND SOMETHING TO EAT.

LET'S SEE...
THE GUN STORE
HOT
GUN
MOM, HOW'D YOU DO THAT SCHOOL-OF-HEAVENS SUMMONING?
IT MUST'VE BEEN THANKS TO YOU, BECAUSE I WAS HOLDING YOU IN MY ARMS.
KALASH
GUN
MOM, YOU KNOW THAT'S NOT HOW IT WORKS.
AH, HERE WE GO. LOOK!

WOW! THOSE ARE THE BOATS YOU WERE TALKING ABOUT?
COME ON, ADRIAN. LET'S GO!

DOCK 4, UNLOADING!
NO ENTERING THE PIER WHILE WE UNLOAD!
MOM, CHECK OUT ALL THOSE BOOKS—I'VE NEVER SEEN SO MANY!
YES.
HEY, WHAT'S THIS?
SEXY
Sirens
SUPER HOT
100% SEX
ADRIAN, PUT THAT DOWN! IT'S NOT FOR...
...KIDS.

BUT...
OH, ALL RIGHT...
I NEVER GET TO DO ANYTHING...
THE ROYAL CUP!

EXCUSE ME...
SIR, THE CUP THAT'S IN-
OH, DEAR, SUCH A BEAUTY!
MY, MY!
YOU MUST'VE FLED A FIVE-STAR ESTABLISHMENT, NO?
A WHAT?
PARDON MY ENTHUSIASM, BUT I DON'T USUALLY SEE PRETTY GIRLS LIKE YOU AROUND HERE.
THAT ROYAL CUP...
THE MAN WHO SOLD IT TO YOU-WAS HE TALL AND BURLY? DARK HAIR?
THE CUP?

NICE PIECE, ISN'T IT? OVER 500 YEARS OLD. UNFORTUNATELY, IT'S ALREADY SPOKEN FOR...
YOU DON'T OFTEN GET SUCH WELL-PRESERVED ARTIFACTS.
LISTEN— MY SON'S NAME IS ENGRAVED ON THAT CUP.
IT BELONGS TO THE VALLEY OF KINGS.
THE VALLEY OF...
HA HA! DON'T WORRY; THAT SORT OF THING ISN'T MUCH OF A CONCERN. NO ONE WILL COMPLAIN.
HIS NAME IS ADRIAN VELBA.
HE WON IT THIS YEAR.
TO BE PERFECTLY HONEST, I LIKE YOU.
THAT'S WHY I'M GIVING YOU 10% OFF THE ENTIRE STORE!
IT'S A GIFT FOR THE WHOLE FAMILY.

WHOA...
THE IGUANA QUEEN!
FORSWEAR ALL PROFANE D
OR UNSEEN, FOR NAUGHT E
THE BREATH OF THE IGUAN

I'M NOT HERE TO BUY IT.
I'M LOOKING FOR THE MAN WHO SOLD IT TO YOU.
AH... THAT?
CHECK THE BARS AND BROTHELS, AND YOU'LL FIND HIM. IF HE ISN'T ROTTING IN JAIL, THAT IS.
HA HA HA!
HEEEY!
THAT'S MY CUP!!!
COME ON, WE'RE LEAVING.
BUT MY CUP...
LET'S GO!
BUT I FOUND A BOOK.

WELL, PUT IT BACK. WE'RE NOT HERE TO-
NO!
ADRIAN...
I WANT THIS BOOK!
YOU WANT THE BOOK?
WHAT'S WITH THE TANTRUM? I TOLD YOU TO PUT IT DOWN!
IT'S NOT FAIR!
EVER SINCE WE'VE LEFT, YOU'RE WALKING NONSTOP, DOING THIS, DOING THAT... BUT I'M NOT ALLOWED TO DO ANYTHING!
BESIDES, THE IGUANA QUEEN'S IN THIS BOOK...
...AND THE BLIND KNIGHT.
SO, YOU REALLY WANT THIS BOOK?
YES.
IT'S NOT JUST A WHIM?
NO. IT TALKS ABOUT THE VALLEY TOO...

HERE, THAT SHOULD BE ENOUGH.
TAC!
REALLY? THE BOOK'S MINE?
YES, IT'S YOURS.
THANKS, MOM.
WHAT, SHE THINKS THAT CRUMMY COIN OF HERS IS ENOUGH TO–
WAIT...
THE LION OF THE VALLEY?!
WHAT DID SHE SAY HIS NAME WAS?
ALEX MELBA?
NO,
IT'S ADR–
A.VELBA
R.ALDAÑA
OH CRAP!

BORG'S
BAR
NO MONEY! GET THE HELL OUT!
I JUST GOT OUTTA PRISON—I NEED SOME LOVIN'!
OVER HERE, BABE.
200 BUCKS, HONEY.
GOOD THING I WENT TO THE BANK!
HE'S BURIED HERE!!!
HA HA!
BOTH OF YOU BURN IN HELL.
50/50 AND THE INTEREST IS MINE.
NO WAY!
LOOKIN' GOOD! HEY, BABE, HOW MUCH D'YA CHARGE?
ADRIAN, HOLD MY HAND.
EXCUSE ME, I'M LOOKING FOR A TALL MAN WITH DARK HAIR AND A WHITE BAG...
RICHARD ALDANA?
ALDANA?
NO, NEVER HEARD OF HIM.
ARE THERE OTHER BARS AROUND HERE?

UM...
THE RUM TAVERN.
AND SO THE CHICK WAS THERE WITH HER KID.
THEN?
THE USUAL. WE STOP HER.
SHOW YOUR ID, WE SAID. THE GIRL DOESN'T HAVE ANY, SO WE FOLLOW THE STANDARD PROTOCOL.
YEAH. SO WE GET HER OFF THE BIKE, OPEN THE BAG...
RAPE.
I GO TAKE THE KID'S HELMET.
AND THEN, GUYS, I SWEAR...
THAT GIRL, SHE...
SHE...
SHE WHAT?
GO ON! WHAT'D SHE DO?

SHE, UH...
SHE HIT ME...
SHE HIT YOU?!
THAT'S CRAZY!
WHAT WAS THIS CHICK LIKE?
WELL, UH...
MAYBE SHE WAS HORNY.
UM...
SHE WAS...
UH...
...
SH!
C'MON! WAS SHE HOT?
REALLY UGLY. BRUNETTE, WITH A SCAR ON HER FACE.
UH, NO, NO...SHORT AND FAT...

MAN, THAT'S ROUGH...YOU KNOW WHAT? YOU SHOULD FILE A COMPLAINT.
I DUNNO.
MOM, THAT'S THE MAN FROM—
YES.
HEY! IT'S HER!!!

...

THE HOOLIGAN...
...WITH HER BRAT...

BEEP-BEEP! THE BITCH WHO ASSAULTED US IN AN UNCONVENTIONAL MANNER! RIGHT THERE!!!
WHICH ONE?!
HER!

THAT'S THE SHORT, FAT, SUPER-UGLY GIRL?
I CAN'T BELIEVE IT! USING HER BEAUTY TO STRIKE AN NPTP AGENT!
WELL, ACTUALLY...
ADRIAN, HAND ME THAT.
BUT MOM...
PROCEED WITH THE ARREST OF THE HOO... HOOL...
BLAM!
MY BOOK!
CLAP!
GOT IT!
BOSS! YOU HURT?
IN THE NAME OF THE LAW, I'LL RIP YOU A NEW ONE!

RUN!

ARREST THEM, GODDAMN IT!!!

WAAAAAH!
HEY!
THIS TIME WE'LL CARRY OUT THE SENTENCE IMMEDIATELY!
HUFF!
TAP
TAP!
TAP!
HA!
THERE! UP AHEAD!

FIVE SECONDS TILL DEPARTURE!
OH!
EXCUSE ME!
HEY!
TAP!
THE ELEVATOR!
KLANG

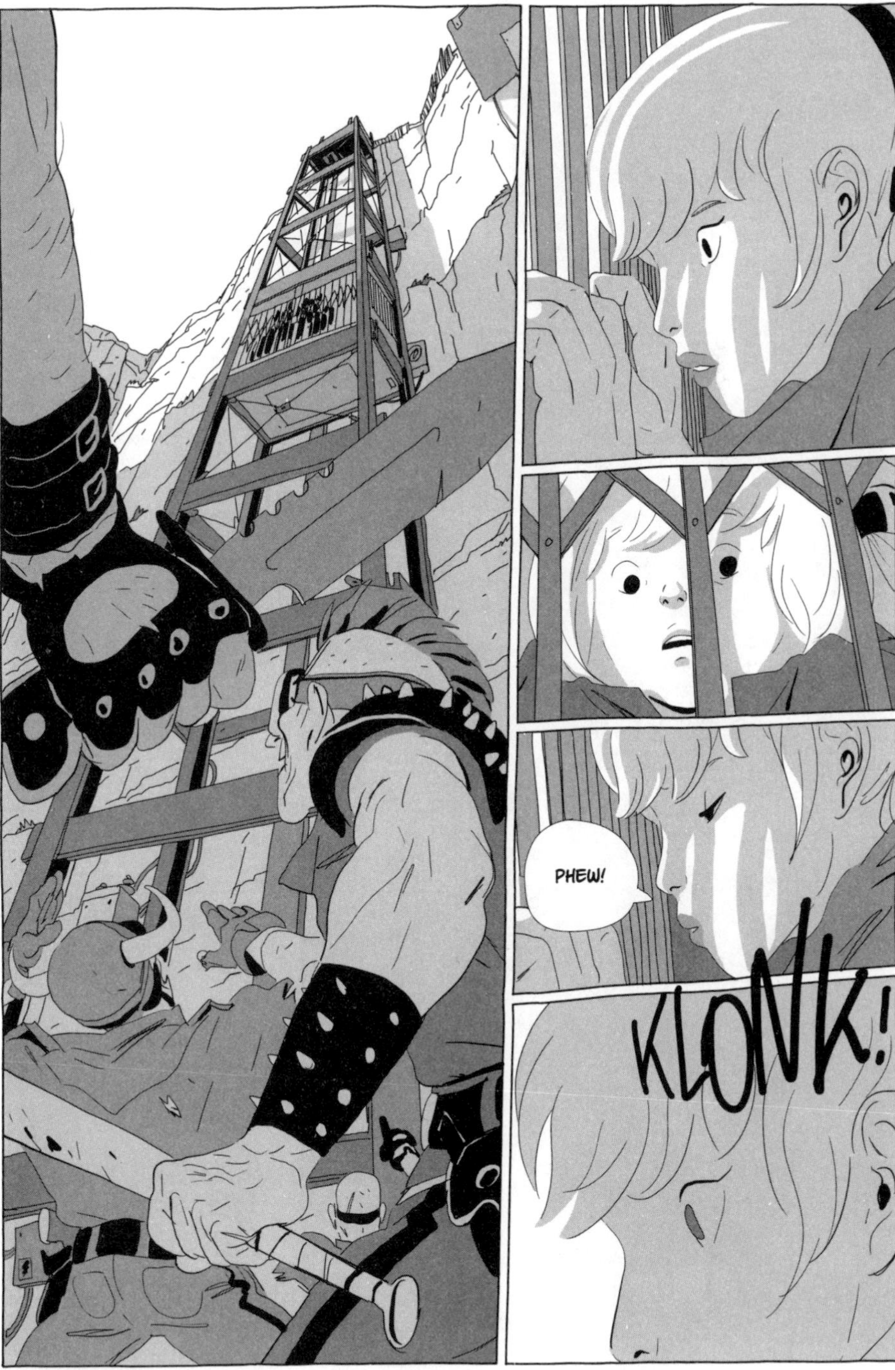
PHEW!
KLONK!

DAMN!
WHAT IS THIS CRAP?
IT'S THOSE APES FROM THE TURBOPOLICE! THEY'VE GONE BERSERK AGAIN!
THIS TIME THEY'RE WRECKING THE ELEVATOR CABLES.
THAT'S A PROBLEM.
KWANG
NOW THEY'RE STARTING IN ON THE COUNTERWEIGHT. WE'RE NOT GOING TO GET FAR.

STAY CALM!
KLANG!
IT'S A GOOD DAY TO DIE, BROTHERS!
DON'T GIVE IN TO FEAR–ACCEPT YOUR DESTINY...
THE TIME HAS COME!
LET US JOIN HANDS, MY FRIENDS...
ADRIAN! WE'VE GOT TO FIND A WAY TO OPEN THIS GATE!
KLINK

KRANG!
SHKR
BOM
BODOM
BOM
HEAR THE DRUMS OF THE APOCALYPSE!
BOM
SHKRAK!
VRRR!
HA HA!
KRAK!

HAVE NO FEAR, CITIZENS OF NILLIPOLIS!
THE FIRE BRIGADE IS HERE!
KRAK!
CRAP! IT'S THE FIREMEN!
KLUNK
WHAT DO WE DO, BOSS?

WE'LL GO ROUND BY THE RING ROAD. THE HOOLIGAN MUST PAY FOR HER CRIMES!!!
THUD
IN THE NAME OF THE LAW!
SO, PATRICK, STILL DESTROYING PUBLIC PROPERTY? THIS TIME I'M ARRESTING YOU!
FIREMEN DON'T HAVE THE AUTHORITY, IDIOT! LET THE POLICE DO THEIR WORK!
POLICE, MY ASS! GO HOME TO YOUR MAMA!
YOU KNOW WHERE YOU CAN STICK THAT FIRE HOSE OF YOURS?
OH YEAH? WHERE?
THERE!
SLAP!
ARGH! IN THE NAME OF THE LAW!
BONK!
HOLD ON TIGHT, ADRIAN!
GO!

ALL DONE, MA'AM. FIRE BRIGADE, AT YOUR SERVICE!
THANKS SO MUCH. IT'S GOOD TO KNOW NOT ALL OF YOU ARE INSANE HERE...
BEEP-BEEP, GUYS!
SLAP
TAP
THERE THEY ARE! GET 'EM!
MOM! THE APES!
WELL, THANKS AGAIN. WE'VE GOTTA RUN. SAY THANK YOU, ADRIAN.
THANKS.

WELCOME, GENTLEMEN!!!
WHAT'LL IT BE?
LOOKING FOR A GOOD TIME?
SHUT THE HELL UP.

THE HOTTEST GIRLS IN TOWN!
BUY TWO DRINKS, GET ONE FREE.
I'M GAY.
HA HA HA HA!
HEY, HANDSOME!
HAVE WE GOT A FUN NIGHT FOR YOU!
NO THANKS, BUDDY.

HMM...IT'S KINDA SLOW TONIGHT.
YOU'RE SAYING YESTERDAY WAS BETTER?
WE'VE GOT A VIRGIN AND A PENNILESS DRUNK IN THE LOUNGE...
...AND THE GIRLS SITTING ON THEIR BUTTS.
YEAH, BUT THINGS ARE GONNA PICK UP AGAIN, I CAN FEEL IT.

YOU CAN FEEL IT, HUH?
WELL, LUCKY YOU–THAT'S ALL I CAN SAY!
ONE LAST DRINK, THEN I'M HEADING HOME...

HEY, IT'S OUR PATRIARCH!
MY FRANCIS...
YOU SEE, FLORA, AS LONG AS WE HAVE MR. JACOBS AS A CUSTOMER, WE'LL STAY IN BUSINESS!
YES, WE HAVE ONE REGULAR CUSTOMER AND YOU GIVE HIM DRINKS ON THE HOUSE.
WOULD YOU BE A DEAR AND OFFER ME A DRINK, FRANCIS?

BUSINESS SENSE REALLY DOESN'T RUN IN YOUR VEINS...
DON'T LISTEN TO HER, MY LITTLE FRANCIS. JUST FIX ME A NICE LIL' SHOT O' RUM!

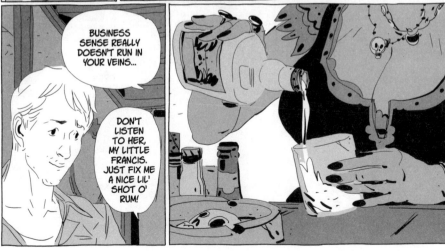

TIMES CHANGE...
...AS DOES THE CLIENTELE.
WE'LL GET BACK ON TOP, I'M SURE.
I'M GONNA STEP OUTSIDE TO DRUM UP SOME BUSINESS.
MMMM...

I'M NOT GONNA LIE, MY LITTLE FRANCIS, THERE WAS A TIME WHEN PEOPLE WERE FIGHTING TO GET IN HERE. BUT IT HAD LESS TO DO WITH YOUR DAD THAN WITH MERILYN.
DAMN! WHERE'D I PUT THAT THING...
HIT ME AGAIN, SWEET-HEART?

AH, MERILYN... WHAT A SAINTLY WOMAN. SHE HAD THIS WAY ABOUT HER, ALWAYS SWEET, ALWAYS GENTLE, BUT GET HER IN BED AND SHE'D DO THESE INCREDIBLE-
YES, WE ALL MISS HER.
SHE WAS THE HEART AND SOUL OF THIS PLACE. THAT'S WHY IT DID SO WELL.
NOT LIKE IT'S DOING NOW, WITH THAT FLORA.
FLORA'S GREAT—WHY WOULD YOU SAY THAT?
SHE HATES ME.

MERILYN! SUCH CHARISMA!
THAT KINDA THING CAN'T BE TAUGHT! AND SO... RESPECTFUL!
UM... I'VE GOTTA HEAD BACK, MR. JACOBS.
LONG BLOND HAIR, STUNNING FACE, THOSE CURVES... YES, SHE WAS BEAUTIFUL ALL RIGHT- THE MOST GORGEOUS ONE OF ALL.
YEAH, FOR SURE, SHE-
HEY!
SO NO HOTEL AFTER...

...ALL?
?
WAIT...
HOLD ON...
VLAM!
OUCH...
ARGH...

WELL, WELL...
WELL, WHADDYA KNOW... IT LOOKS LIKE WE HAVE SOME SERIOUS GUESTS, LADIES...
DRINKS, GENTLEMEN?
HEH HEH...
...
TELL ME AGAIN!

A WOMAN AND KID...
...PAYING WITH THAT KINDA COIN? YEAH, I SAW 'EM.
AND HER VEHICLE?
UH...
AN OLD YELLOW MOTORCYCLE. ROW 20.
AND SHE PAID FOR INSURANCE...
SO TRY FOR LESS DAMAGE THIS TIME, REYNOLDS.
NO WORRIES! I'LL LOOK AFTER IT.

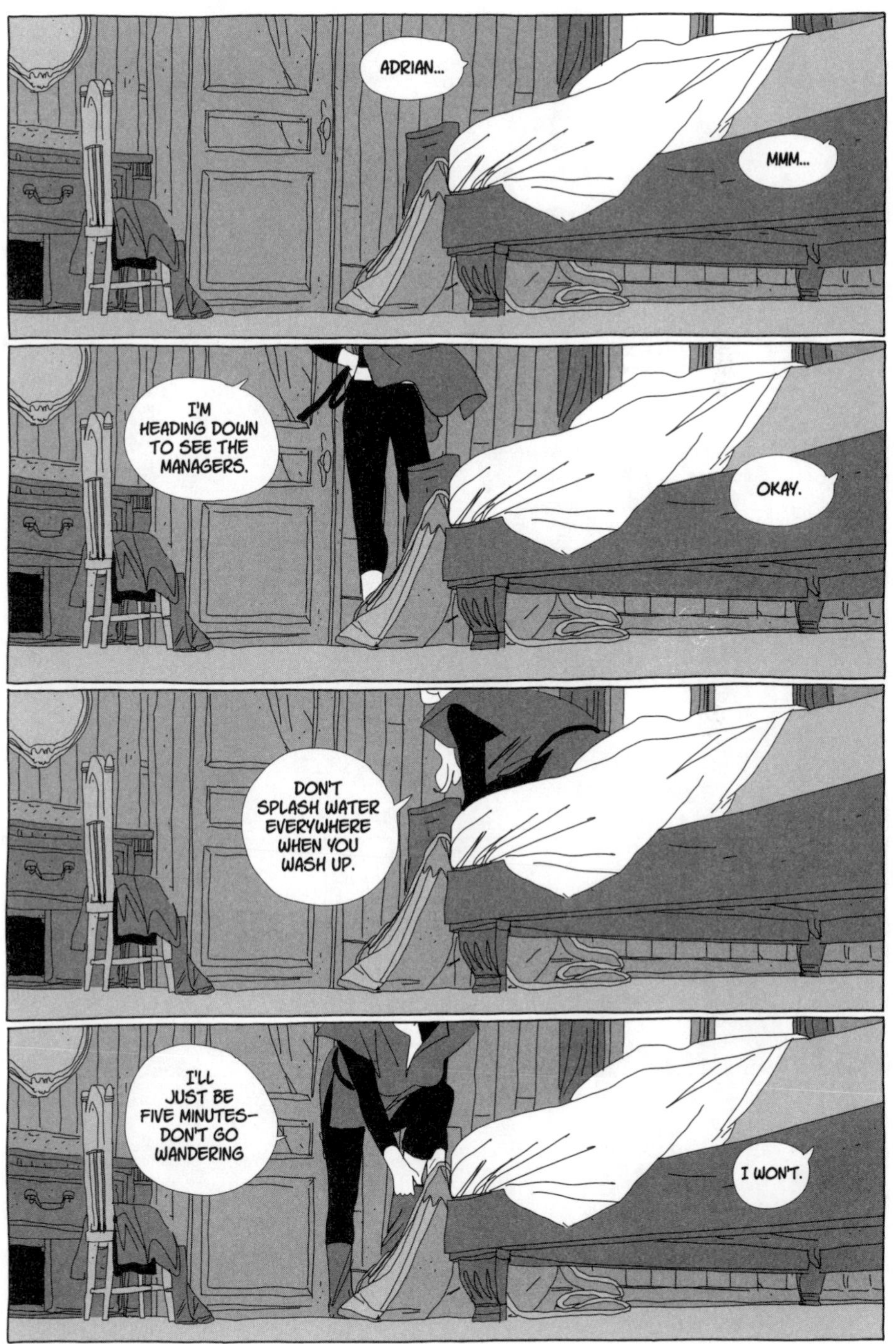
ADRIAN...
MMM...
I'M HEADING DOWN TO SEE THE MANAGERS.
OKAY.
DON'T SPLASH WATER EVERYWHERE WHEN YOU WASH UP.
I'LL JUST BE FIVE MINUTES– DON'T GO WANDERING
I WON'T.

AH, MARIANNE! YOU'RE UP.
GOOD MORNING, FRANCIS.
I HOPE YOU FOUND THE BEDDING COMFORTABLE.
YES, THE BEDDING WAS FINE.
THE WALLS, THOUGH... THEY'RE A LITTLE THIN.
THE WA— OH, RIGHT. SORRY ABOUT THAT...
ANYWAY, THANKS FOR EVERYTHING.
ARE YOU JOKING? THANK *YOU*. IF YOU HADN'T COME, WE WOULDN'T—
HEY, FRANCIS, I'D LIKE TO WASH A FEW THINGS—
NO PROBLEM! I WAS JUST HEADED TO THE LAUNDRY ROOM NOW, ACTUALLY.
ALL THAT TRAVELING, YOU KNOW...
YES, OF COURSE!

THANKS TO YOU, WE HAD A FULL HOUSE—EVERY ROOM WAS BOOKED.
IT'S UNHEARD OF!
WE CAN RESTART THE BUSINESS, WE MADE SO MUCH LAST NIGHT. IT'S A MIRACLE.
YOU'RE WELCOME.
I KNOW THIS ISN'T EXACTLY AN APPROPRIATE PLACE FOR CHILDREN...
YOU MEAN MY SON? OH, DON'T WORRY—HE KNOWS HOW TO FEND FOR HIMSELF.
REALLY?
HE WON THE ROYAL CUP.
THE ROYAL CUP?

WHAT IS IT? BOXING?
OH YEAH? WHERE?
PAST THE DESERT, IN THE VALLEY.
THE VALLEY?
SOMETHING LIKE THAT.
THAT'S SURPRISING. YOU KNOW, ALL THE GREATEST CHAMPIONS USED TO COME CELEBRATE THEIR WINS HERE. MY DAD WOULD WELCOME THEM, AND–
OH, THE CUP TAKES PLACE IN ANOTHER CITY.
FRANCIS–I'VE BEEN MEANING TO ASK YOU... I'M LOOKING FOR A MAN.
A MAN?
FOR?
KIND OF TALL AND BURLY, DARK HAIR, SLIGHT BEARD, BLACK JACKET WITH A BAG ON HIS SHOULDER. HE MAY HAVE COME THROUGH HERE.
YOU WANT ME TO ASK THE GIRLS? THEY'D KNOW FAR BETTER THAN ME.

THAT'D BE GREAT-THANKS.
AND THE WASH...?
YES, RIGHT, HAND ME YOUR THINGS.
HERE...
I BROUGHT ADRIAN'S TOO.
AND CRU... CRUCIFERA EMERGED FROM THE FLOWER...
CRUCIFERA CHOPS UP THE THREE KNIGHTS.
ITS PETALS TURNED RED, SOAKED BY THE BLOOD OF THE KNIGHTS SHE SLAYED...
THE THREE KNIGHTS OF THE GUAR
THEIR LIMBS RENT FRO
AS THE

NOT EVEN THE ROYAL GUARD COULD STOP CRUCIFERA...
CRUCIFERA...
HEY, MIDGET!
?!
BEEP-BEEP...
BEEP...BEEP!

OH NO! THE CRAZY GUY!

AREN'T YOU A LITTLE YOUNG TO BE HANGING OUT IN A BROTHEL?
GET OUT OF HERE!

LIEUTENANT! WAKE UP THE TEAM! LAW AND ORDER CAN'T WAIT.

COME ON BACK SOMETIME— AND BRING YOUR FRIENDS!

YOU LOST YOUR MOM, HON?
IS ANYONE LOOKING AFTER YOU?

...
IT'S COFFEE. GO ON, TAKE A SIP.

CRUCIFERA... THE...WITCH...
WHAT?
DID YOU REALLY JUST CALL ME A WITCH?
ADRIAN!
...

LOOK–FRANCIS LENT US SOME CLOTHES.
WOMEN IN SAILORS' OUTFITS? IS THAT A THING NOW?
HERE, PUT THIS ON INSTEAD OF YOUR PJ's.
NO, I DON'T WANNA GET NAKED HERE.
IT'S JUST FOR WHILE OUR CLOTHES DRY.
I'M MARIANNE, BY THE WAY.
PFFF...
I GOTTA SAY, MARIANNE...YOU WON'T GET MANY CUSTOMERS IN THAT GETUP.
FINE BY ME! I'M A BAKER, SO...
NO, NO, THAT'S NOT WHAT FLORA MEANT...
FRANCIS!

FRANCIS!

THE TOADS ARE OUT FRONT!

NO ONE COMES IN, NO ONE GOES OUT!

INSPECT ALL WORK PERMITS!

DBA

LET'S SEE 'EM, LADIES! WILL THE OWNER OF THE PREMISES PLEASE STEP FORWARD!

PAF!

TBA

UM... THAT'D BE ME!

BUT WE HAD OUR INSPECTION LAST MONTH...

TAP!

LISTEN, I'M NOT A P—

BOSS!

WHERE ARE YOU HIDING HER?

IT'S HER! NO PAPERS!
LET GO OF ME! I KEEP TELLING YOU— I'M A BAKER, NOT A PROSTITUTE!
SPLENDID! WE'LL TAKE HER AND THE KID!
WHAT?!
LISTEN, I THINK THERE'S BEEN A MISUNDERSTANDING.
SURELY WE CAN WORK SOMETHING OUT.
ENOUGH!
SLAM!
KEEP YOUR HANDS TO YOURSELF, BUDDY!
OKAY, GUYS— CLEAR OUT THE CASH REGISTER.
WHAT?

THE MONEY? IS HE OUT OF HIS MIND?
NOT IN THE LEAST!
CONFISCATE EVERYTHING.
THAT'S ABUSE OF POWER!
WE *EARNED* THAT MONEY!
WITH THE SWEAT OF YOUR LITTLE ASSES? VERY TRUE!
TAKE HER TOO!
STOP IT!
GRAB!
FRANCIS! DO SOMETHING!
HOW ABOUT IT, FRANCIS?

IN THE VAN—NOW!

AND PLEASE, DON'T MAKE A FUSS.

YOU ANIMALS!

FLORA!

BOM

HEY!

BOM BOM BOM

THUMP!

BEAT IT!

THUD!

VROOOOO
MOVE, DAMN IT!
GO ON, ADRIAN. CLIMB UP.
MARIANNE! I'LL FIX THIS!!!
GET OUT OF HERE!
I'LL MEET YOU OVER THERE!

FRANCIS! WHAT ARE YOU DOING?!
I'LL BE BACK!

ARE YOU *KIDDING?* WE WORKED ALL NIGHT FOR NOTHING! YOU'D BETTER GET US OUR MONEY!

LIKE I SAID: I'LL BE BACK.

BWREEEEET
PINK PANTIE

BRAAAA, AAAA
PLEASE LISTEN! I'M NOT THE PERSON YOU'RE LOOKING FOR.
AAARRR
YOU'RE MAKING A MISTAKE!
NO!
THIS IS NO MISTAKE...
...MRS. VELBA.

ALLOW ME TO INTRODUCE MYSELF: I AM ATTORNEY RAVEN, AND THIS IS MY COLLEAGUE...ATTORNEY DELACRUZ.
WE ARE HERE TO DEFEND THE INTERESTS OF OUR BEAUTIFUL CITY OF NILLIPOLIS.
SCREEE
HOW DO YOU KNOW MY NAME?

LET'S SEE WHAT WE HAVE HERE...
DATES. WHATEVER.
HEY— THAT'S MY BAG!
A FEW GOLD COINS.
FOR A GREAT TRAVELER...
YOU'RE SADLY ILL-EQUIPPED!
NO COMPASS, NO GPS...
TELL ME, MRS. VELBA...

...DOES THE NAME RICHARD ALDANA MEAN ANYTHING TO YOU?

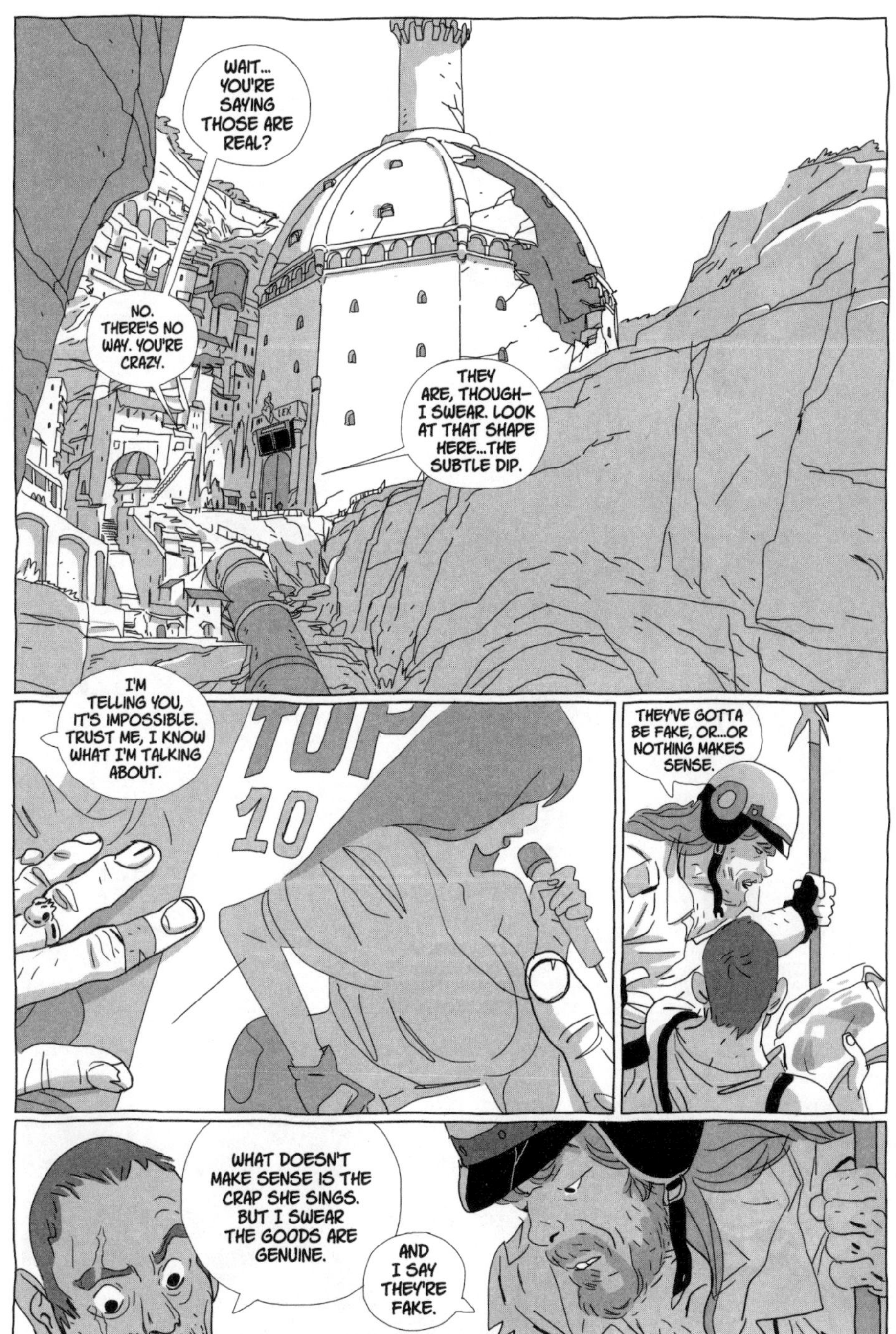
WAIT... YOU'RE SAYING THOSE ARE REAL?
NO. THERE'S NO WAY. YOU'RE CRAZY.
THEY ARE, THOUGH— I SWEAR. LOOK AT THAT SHAPE HERE...THE SUBTLE DIP.
I'M TELLING YOU, IT'S IMPOSSIBLE. TRUST ME, I KNOW WHAT I'M TALKING ABOUT.
TOP 10
THEY'VE GOTTA BE FAKE, OR...OR NOTHING MAKES SENSE.
WHAT DOESN'T MAKE SENSE IS THE CRAP SHE SINGS. BUT I SWEAR THE GOODS ARE GENUINE.
AND I SAY THEY'RE FAKE.

THEY'RE REAL. TRUST ME.
Post
AND HOW THE HELL WOULD YOU KNOW? YOU HER DAD OR SOMETHING?
DOESN'T MATTER.
SO TELL ME, GENTLEMEN...
THESE ARE THE RESULTS OF YESTERDAY'S TRIAL, CORRECT?
THAT? WELL, YEAH!
SEE THIS MAN UP HERE?
THE ARTICLE MENTIONS A TRANSFER BUT GIVES NO DATE...
HEE HEE! YEAH, THAT GUY'S STILL HERE. HIS DEFENSE GOT BLOWN TO BITS–NOT A PRETTY SIGHT.
REALLY.
YEAH. NO SURPRISE, THOUGH. HE HAD RAVEN AND DELACRUZ FACING HIM, THE TWO BEST LAWYERS IN TOWN.

WELL, SPEAK OF THE DEVILS...
THAT'S THEM OVER THERE, WITH JUDGE WINCHESTER. IT SEEMS THEY'VE GOTTEN THEMSELVES SOME NEW CLIENTS.
FROM THE LOOK ON HER FACE, I'D SAY SHE'S DEFINITELY NO CLIENT OF THEIRS!
WHY, HELLO, MY GOOD MAN!
YOUR HONOR, COUNSELORS...ARE YOU HERE FOR AN EXPRESS PROCEDURE?
WHAT NAME SHOULD I PUT IT UNDER, YOUR HONOR?
MARIANNE VELBA, IF YOU PLEASE.
DOWN

5 P.M. WOULD BE GOOD.
YOU GOT THIS, BUDDY?
YUP, NILLIPOLIS VERSUS V-E-L-B...
TAP TAP TAP CLACK CLACK
GAME ON!
BOND-MAX
HUMUNGUS
TCHAK TCHAK
TCHAC
NILLIPOLIS-VELBA
TCHAK
THERE'S A CELL FOR YOUR USE, IN THE BASEMENT.
WOW! WHAT A BOMBSHELL!
SURE IS! SO, MR. EXPERT... WERE THOSE REAL?
HEY, WHERE'D HE GO?

WOOO!
OWW!!
WAAA!
GRRR!
YAAAAR!
WOO!
WOO!
CRiii
WOO!
WOO!
WOOO!
HEY, SEXY!
SEXY!
TSSS!
TSS!!
...
OKAY, MOVE IT ALONG.

SHUT YER FACES IF YA DON'T WANT SOLITARY!
WORK IT, BABE!
LOOK AHEAD, ADRIAN.
JUST IGNORE THEM...
HEY, KID?
KID,
IS THAT YOUR MAMA?
SHE'S HOT.
DOES YOUR MAMA WANT TO COME PLAY IN MY CELL?
COME ON!
THERE'S ROOM ON MY LAP IF YOU WANNA COME TOO.
CLACK!
KLANG!
ADRIAN, YOU HEARD WHAT THEY SAID! RICHARD'S IN NILLIPOLIS...
HE'S CLOSE BY—I'M SURE OF IT.

I'M SO SORRY, SWEETIE...
SO, TELL ME: WHAT'S IN YOUR BOOK?
I'M READING ABOUT THE GREAT ROOSTER.
Faligule
M EDGE OF THE
FOREST, HE CAN
ONLY SPELL BY
HICH THE KING
SO YOU'VE BEEN READING THE TEXT?
WELL, NOT THE PARTS WITH SMALL LETTERS.
HE'S PRETTY IMPRESSIVE.
AND LOOK...
HERE'S CRUCIFERA. SHE'S MY FAVORITE.

HMPF.
HUFF...
HUFF...
Guard Post

OKAY, FRANCIS, THINK...
THE CELLS.
HOW DO YOU GET TO THE BASEMENT?

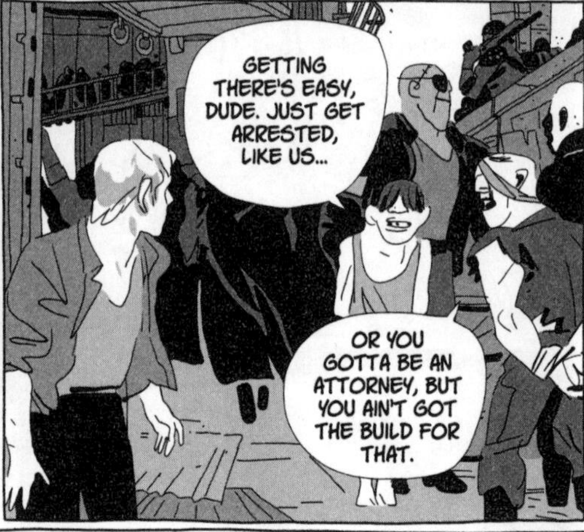
GETTING THERE'S EASY, DUDE. JUST GET ARRESTED, LIKE US...
OR YOU GOTTA BE AN ATTORNEY, BUT YOU AIN'T GOT THE BUILD FOR THAT.

THERE'S BEEN A MISTAKE...INNOCENT PEOPLE ARE IN JAIL.

INNOCENT—HA! YOU WON'T BE SEEING THEM AGAIN. AT LEAST YOU CAN WATCH RAVEN AND DELACRUZ PLEADING IN THE GREAT HALL AT 5:00.
IT'S HIGH-CALIBER LAWYERING!

TONIGHT / 5PM
NILLIPOLIS
VS
VELBA
JUDGE

SHOULD BE A NICE BLOODBATH.

A BLOODBATH...
GZZ...
GZZ...
AND...GZZ... A MAP?
NO...
EVERYTHING FROM INSIDE THE BAG IS HERE.
HEH HEH...
THAT SAID, THERE ARE A FEW INTERESTING THINGS...

INTEREST-GZZ-ING THINGS?

SOME COINS AND...GZZ... DRIED FRUIT.

NO ONE TRAVELS WITHOUT A MAP! SHE MUST... GZZ...STILL HAVE IT ON HER.

YOU SAID THE SAME THING ABOUT THAT... GZZ...OTHER ONE...
ROBERT BANANA...
RICHARD ALDANA.
AFTER THE... GZZ...TRIAL AND THE...GZZ... INCARCERATION, YOU HAD NOTHING!

ALDANA'S ABOUT AS TOUGH AS THEY COME. WE CRUSHED HIM IN COURT–EASILY– BUT...
...NO ONE CAN GET HIM TO TALK.

SO, TO SUM UP... GZZ... NO MAP, NO CONFESSION, BUT...GZZ... ALL IS WELL.

WITHOUT THE OTHER HALF OF THE MAP, I SHOULD...GZZ... REMIND YOU THAT I'M...GZZ... FINISHED.
NO, NO– IMPOSSIBLE!
YOU'RE LOOKING GREAT.

WHY THIS... GZZ... LACK OF PROGRESS?
MAYBE BECAUSE THE "VALLEY OF KINGS" IS A CHILDREN'S FAIRY TALE...
WHAT?

WHAT DID HE JUST SAY?
NOTHING, NOTHING. JUST THAT...UM... THE VALLEY OF KINGS IS CLOSER THAN EVER.
THAT BETTER BE IT!
THE VALLEY OF... GZZ... KINGS.
THE LAND WHERE PEOPLE STAY YOUNG... GZZ... FOREVER...
I NEED ONLY ...GZZ...SET FOOT IN THAT GLORIOUS PLACE...
...AND I WILL BE SAVED...
DEATH HAS BEEN VANQUISHED THERE...THAT'S WHY THE VALLEY IS HIDDEN...
SOME THINK IT'S...GZZ... LONG BEEN DESTROYED, OR...GZZ... NEVER EXISTED...
BUT IT ***DOES*** EXIST.
WRAPPED IN THE WARM BREATH OF THE IGUANA...
HOPE SPRINGS ETERNAL.
WHAT WAS THAT HE SAID?
NO, NO, NOTHING! GNN!!!
GET THAT GIRL TO TALK AT THE TRIAL, AND YOUR PAYMENT... WILL GROW...
LIKE THESE TUMORS GROWING IN MY HEAD...

FAKE!
REAL!
REAL!
FAKE!
UM...

IF THOSE ARE REAL, THEY CAN HANG ME BY THE...
THEY'RE REAL!
YEAH, WELL, MUSIC-WISE TOMIE KATANA'S NOT THAT HOT.
EXCUSE ME.
JAIL = FREEDOM
WHO CARES?

EXCUSE ME, SIR? WOULD IT BE POSSIBLE FOR ME TO...
GOOD POINT.
...UM...VISIT DETAINEES?

YOU A LAWYER?
NO.
RELATIVE?
UH...

...
YES.
WELL, I...
HEY, GUYS!

CHECK IT OUT!
TOMIE KATANA... NAKED.

SERIOUSLY?
BROUGHT OVER THIS MORNING BY A SAILOR ON A CARGO SHIP COMING IN FROM PAXTOWN.
DAAAAMN!
YOU SEE! THERE'S NO DOUBT!

OH YEAH, THOSE ARE REAL!
UH, HELLO? THERE'S BEEN A MISTAKE...
THEY'VE HAD THIS FOR TWO WEEKS IN PAXTOWN.
WHILE WE, OF COURSE, CAN JUST ROT.
NILLIPOLIS REALLY IS A DUMP.

WHADDAYA WANT, KID?
UM... I HAVE TO SEE PRISONERS VELBA AND...
I'M IN LOVE!
WELL, WHY DIDN'T YA SAY SO! HAND ME THE KEYS, BIG GUY!
YEAH, YEAH...
SHE'S AN ANGEL...

HEY, YOU DONE DROOLING ON THAT?
IT'S A COLLECTOR'S EDITION.
THEN WE'VE GOTTA MAKE PHOTOCOPIES.
OKAY, GENTLEMEN, I'LL LEAVE IT WITH YOU. BUT IT BETTER BE PRISTINE WHEN I GET BACK.

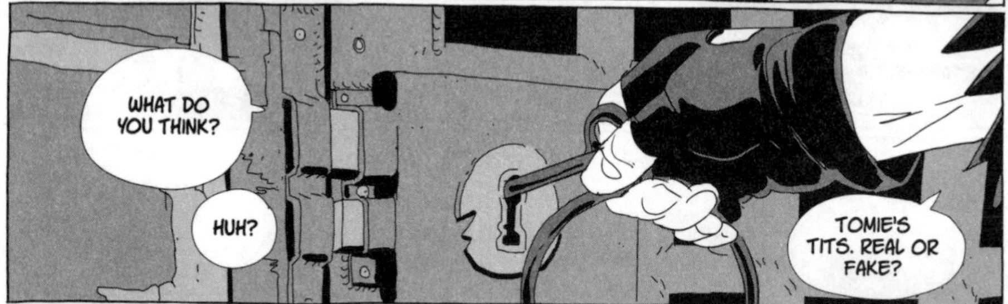
WHAT DO YOU THINK?
HUH?
TOMIE'S TITS. REAL OR FAKE?

NO IDEA.
I SAY IT DOESN'T MATTER.

THE VELBA TRIAL'S AT 5:00, RIGHT?
HAAA
NICE ASS!
THAT'S WHY I HAVE TO SEE THEM RIGHT AWAY.

I'M WORRIED ABOUT THE BOY. HE'S A BIT YOUNG FOR THIS PLACE.

HAAR HA WHOO!
YOU GUYS CLOSE?

UM, NO... LET'S JUST SAY HIS MOTHER REMINDS ME OF SOMEONE I KNEW A LONG TIME AGO...

THEY'RE PRETTY SPECIAL!
TO SAY THE LEAST!

HEY, SKIPPER, I'VE GOT SOMETHING SPECIAL RIGHT HERE!
MEOW...
HERE WE ARE.
506B
MARIANNE! ADRIAN!

IT'S ME! FRANCIS!
WAIT, THIS ISN'T-
THUNK!
BOOM!
THUD!
HEH HEH!
MY POOR RICHARD, WHAT MESS HAVE YOU GOTTEN YOURSELF INTO NOW?

HEAR, HEAR, JUSTICE-LOVING CITIZENS!
WE'VE GOT A LOVELY EVENING PLANNED FOR YOU!
TO START, A SORDID RAPE CASE IN COURTROOM B. KRISTI VERSUS SPECK!
ONLY 20 SEATS LEFT!
AND THEN...
IN COURTROOM A, THE TRIAL OF THE DAY: RAVEN AND DELACRUZ VERSUS VELBA THE FELONIOUS PROSTITUTE!
...GIVE IT UP FOR THE JUSTICE GIRLS!
THE TRIAL WILL BEGIN IN TWENTY MINUTES. HURRY UP AND GRAB THOSE SEATS!
01

STRIP! STRIP!
TUR...
TUR...
TUR...
TURBO-JUSTICE!
PRESIDING OVER THE TRIAL, YOUR FAVORITE MAGISTRATE... JUDGE WINCHESTER!
BAM!
SILENCE!

TODAY HIS HONOR WILL BE JUDGING THE FOLLOWING TWO CASES:
THE STATE VERSUS MARIANNE VELBA, FOR THE FRAUD OF WORKING AS AN UNREGISTERED WHORE...
...AND THE STATE VERSUS BEATRICE BURKETT, A.K.A FLORA, FOR INSULTING MAGISTRATES AND LAW-ENFORCEMENT PERSONNEL.
WHOA, THOSE ARE SOME BADASS CHICKS!
WE SHALL NOW BRING IN THE ACCUSED!

BE SEATED!
WHY ARE THERE SO MANY PEOPLE?
BECAUSE THAT'S HOW PROBLEMS ARE SOLVED IN THIS CESSPOOL OF DEGENERATES!

AND YET AGAIN, FRANCIS LETS ME DOWN.

I CALL THE ACCUSED TO THE STAND!
YOU MAY APPROACH THE BENCH!

MRS. VELBA—
YOU STAND BEFORE THE NILLIPOLIS SUPREME COURT, ACCUSED OF THE FOLLOWING CRIMES:

FRAUDULENT PRACTICE OF UNREGISTERED PROSTITUTION...

AGGRAVATED ASSAULT ON LAW-ENFORCEMENT PERSONNEL... AND EVADING ARREST...

THESE ARE SERIOUS CHARGES, BUT...

I DON'T SEE YOUR...

MY ATTORNEY?!

FRANCIS! WHERE THE HELL ARE YOU?

...ATTORNEY.

NO ATTORNEY? VERY WELL!

REPRESENTING THE CITY OF NILLIPOLIS, LET US NOW BRING IN...

CHOP CHOP CHOP CHOP CHOP CHOP CHOP

ATTORNEY RAVEN...

CHOP CHOP

...AND ATTORNEY DELACRUZ!

WOOO! DELACRUZ! RAVEN!
YAAAAA
HEE HEE...
VERY WELL...
MRS VELBA... WITHOUT AN ATTORNEY, YOU COULD BE HEADED STRAIGHT TO PRISON.
UNLESS YOU'RE PLANNING TO...
REPRESENT YOURSELF?
YOU BET I AM!
THIS IS AN OUTRAGE! THE W-
NO!

SILENCE!

THROW THAT WHORE IN THE CLINKER FOR CONTEMPT OF COURT!

WHEE...

LET GO OF ME, YOU GOONS!

COME OVER HERE!

FLORA!

STOP!

STOP IT!
FLORA HASN'T DONE ANYTHING! YOU DON'T HAVE THE RIGHT TO THROW HER IN JAIL!
MY MOM HASN'T DONE ANYTHING EITHER!
HEY, KID, SHUT UP!
LET GO OF ME!
MY MOM'S NOT A PROSTITROOT!
GNNN!
EVERYONE CALM DOWN, PLEASE.

ONE NIGHT OF PLEASURE TO WHOEVER REPRESENTS MARIANNE VELBA!
HA HA HA!
PFF! YOU THINK WE'RE NUTS?
WHO HAS A DEATH WISH?
HUH...
SO THAT'S WHAT THE MEN OF NILLIPOLIS AMOUNT TO!
A BUNCH OF BALL-LESS WONDERS!
YOU MAKE ME SICK!
ME!!!

I WEEELL DEEEFEND THE WOMAN'S CASE!
AND I SHALL WEEEN!
FOR I AM ULRICO!
THE LADY AND HER BABY—LET ME PLEAD FOR THEM!
MRS. VELBA, THIS SEEMS MOST FORTUNATE!
LET GO!
BASTARDS!
FLORA...

TELL ME EVERYTHEEENG, MADAM.
YOU CAN TELL ME.

WONDERFUL. ULRICO, YOU HAVE THE FLOOR.
ACCUSED, BE SEATED.

HUM, HUM...
THANK YOU, YOUR HONOR.
HUM...

YOUR NAME AGAIN?
MARIANNE VELBA.
OKAY, PERFECTO.

YOUR HONOR...
MRS. VELBA IS INNOCENT, BECAUSE...

OBJECTION!
KRAAK

SUSTAINED!
ATTORNEY RAVEN HAS THE FLOOR!
WOOOOOOOOOOOO..
YOUR HONOR...
MRS. VELBA—THE ACCUSED—PRACTICES PROSTITUTION WITHOUT A PERMIT!
OBJECTION!
MY CLIENT EEZ NOT A PROSTITUTE. SHE EEZ WEARING SAILOR'S CLOTHES.
PARDON ME, YOUR HONOR...
LIES!
A MERE DISGUISE TO MASK HER PARTICIPATION IN A LUCRATIVE BUSINESS.
BLAM!
THIS IS INSANE.
UGH!
BLAM!
AND SHE PRACTICES IT IN FRONT OF HER CHILD.

THE QUESTION MUST BE ASKED! IS THIS HOW A MOTHER EDUCATES HER CHILD?
WITH SEX? LIES? EVEN THEFT? SHE DID THEM ALL. THIS OLD MAN YOU SEE HERE, THE ONE IN THIS WHEELCHAIR... SHE STOLE THE PROPERTY OF THIS OLD MAN.
IT'S...GZZZ...TRUE, SHE ROBBED ME! ME...AN ELDERLY AND SICK OLD MAN. SHE STOLE MY ANCIENT COINS.
OH, A DISABLED MAN!
WHAT A BITCH!
SHAMEFUL!
AN IRRESPONSIBLE MOTHER, WHO DRAGGED HER SON INTO HER SICK LIFESTYLE!
HOW SAD, REALLY.
PLEASE BRING OUT EXHIBIT 1 FOR THE PROSECUTION.
THIS IS THE PURSE THAT THE ACCUSED WAS CARRYING AT THE TIME OF HER ARREST.
AND, OH! HOW SURPRISING! IT'S FULL OF ANCIENT COINS!
OOOH!
THAT'S MY MONEY...
I EARNED IT HONESTLY, AS A BAKER!
IS THAT THE SLANG FOR "SEX WORKER" THESE DAYS?

NO COMMENT, ULRICO?
WARGL
FINE. PROCEED, COUNSELOR.
...
HHHH
HUA
EXHIBIT 2... A PARKING TICKET.
GNNR!
A WHAT?
I YIELD THE FLOOR TO MY PARTNER!
UMF!
THE ACCUSED REFUSED TO YIELD TO A TRAFFIC STOP BY THE NILLIPOLIS TURBOPOLICE. THE VEHICLE DESCRIBED IN THE CASE FILE MATCHES HERS.
GARGL!
TCHAK
WE ASK FOR THE MAXIMUM SENTENCE!

LET GO OF THIS MAN!
YES—WE CROSSED THE DESERT!
WE COME FROM THE VALLEY OF KINGS!
VERY FUNNY! NEXT YOU'LL BE SAYING YOU'RE FROM WONDERLAND!
HA HA HA HA HA HA
BUT IT'S THE TRUTH!
...
PROVE IT!

I...
WE FOLLOWED AN OLD MAP!
BZZT.
IS THAT SO?
CLERK, DID YOU COME ACROSS ANY MAP?
NOPE. NO SIGN OF A MAP IN THE SLUT'S HANDBAG!
LIARS!
ARE YOU ACCUSING THE NILLIPOLIS SUPREME COURT OF LYING?
IF YOUR LAWYER DOES NOT SURVIVE HIS PLEADING...
IT'LL BE THE DEATH PENALTY FOR YOU AND YOUR SON!
MOM!
THEY'RE COMPLETELY NUTS!
GET AHOLD OF YOURSELF!

I WILL REPRESENT MYSELF!
MY LAWYER IS FIRED!
WOO
WOOOOOOO!
REQUEST GRANTED!
MOM...
NOT NOW, ADRIAN!
ULRICO, YOU ARE NO LONGER ON THIS CASE. ***DISMISSED!***
SPLAT!
YOU HAVE THE FLOOR, MRS. VELBA!

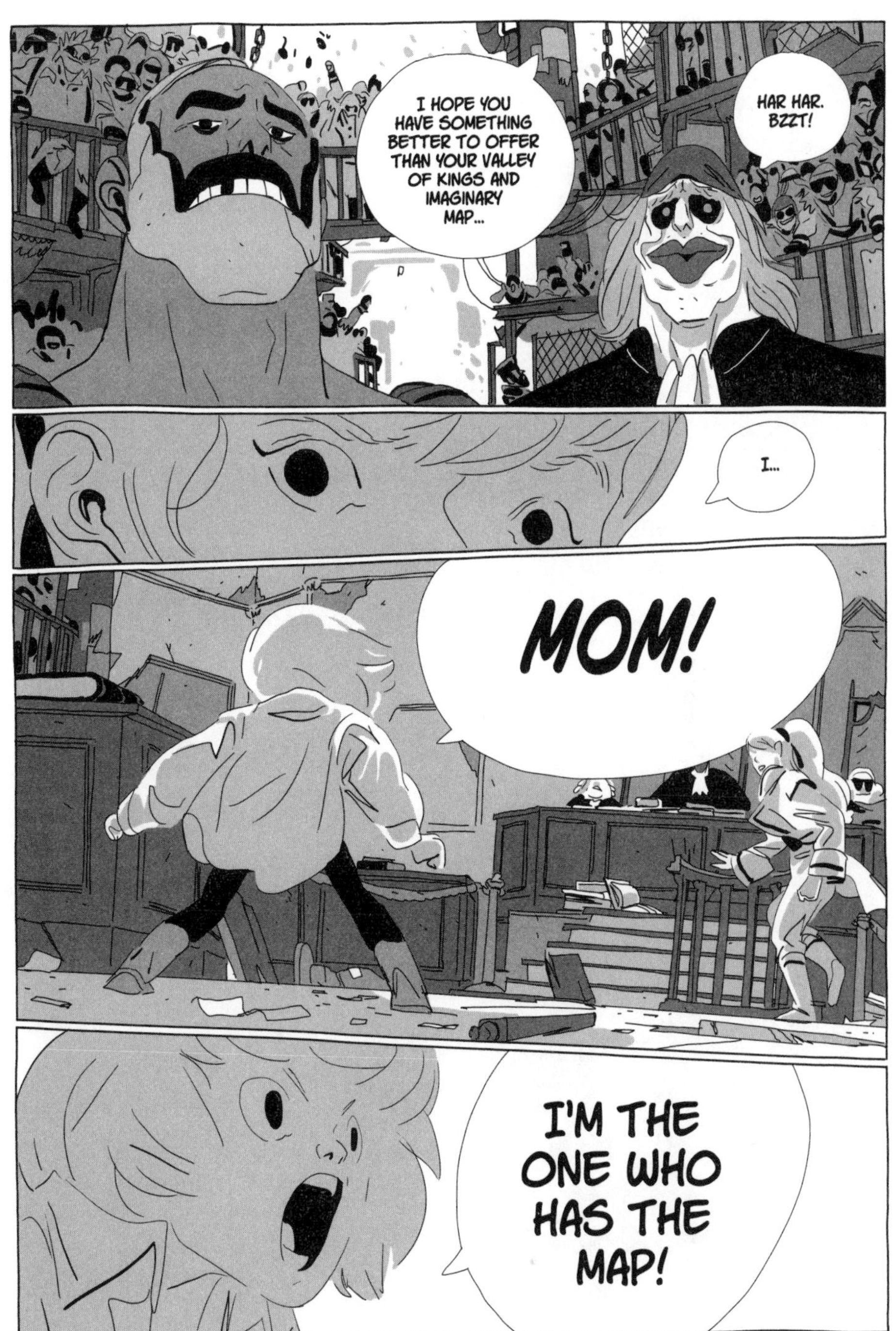
I HOPE YOU HAVE SOMETHING BETTER TO OFFER THAN YOUR VALLEY OF KINGS AND IMAGINARY MAP...
HAR HAR. BZZT!
I...
MOM!
I'M THE ONE WHO HAS THE MAP!

I PUT IT IN THE BOOK!
THANK THE GODS!
GZZT... MY MAP! GZZ...
IT'S MY MAP! SHE STOLE IT FROM ME!
CAUGHT RED-HANDED! CONFISCATE IT!
ALREADY DONE!

KRAK!
TAP
FAST REFLEXES!
MY MAAAAP!
DZ/
WITCH!
YOU'RE LYING! I'VE NEVER SEEN YOU BEFORE!
THAT MAP IS MINE, THIEF!
REALLY? IN THAT CASE...

...EXPLAIN HOW I HAVE THE OTHER HALF!
THE OTHER HALF OF...
...MY MAP!
VOK

THE COURT HAS HEARD ENOUGH! IT IS TIME TO CARRY OUT THE SENTENCE!
TAP
COUNSELOR, IF YOU PLEASE...
INCOMING!
WOOOOOG

WHERE
DID YOU GET
THIS MAP?

GZZ...
WELL, I...
ANSWER ME!
YOU ARE THE ONE WHO MUST ANSWER, DEFENDANT VELBA!
DZZZZZIT
DX
DX

DEATH SENTENCE!
AAAARGH
GZZZ... WATCH OUT! MY MAAAAAP!

FSHHHHHHHHHHH
WHERE'D SHE GO?
PSHHHHHHHHH!
FOOL..

REAL!
FAKE!

INTACT! A MIRACLE!!!
GZZT!
MISSED.
TAP!
SIR, PLEASE SHOW ME THAT MAP!
NO! GZZ... THE MAP IS MINE! THE VALLEY IS MINE!

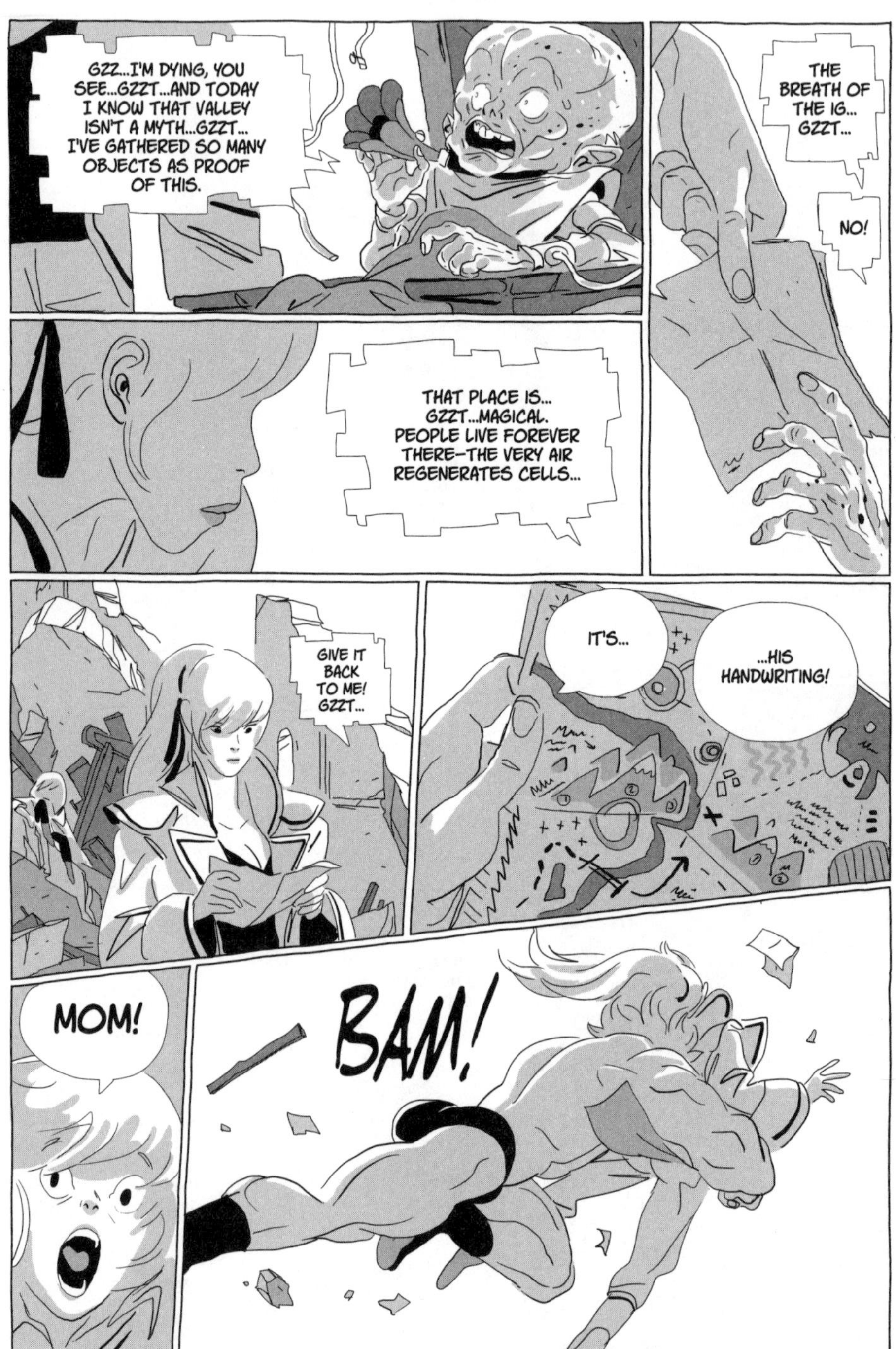
GZZ...I'M DYING, YOU SEE...GZZT...AND TODAY I KNOW THAT VALLEY ISN'T A MYTH...GZZT... I'VE GATHERED SO MANY OBJECTS AS PROOF OF THIS.
THE BREATH OF THE IG... GZZT...
NO!
THAT PLACE IS... GZZT...MAGICAL. PEOPLE LIVE FOREVER THERE—THE VERY AIR REGENERATES CELLS...
GIVE IT BACK TO ME! GZZT...
IT'S...
...HIS HANDWRITING!
MOM!
BAM!

AGGRAVATED ASSAULT ON MY CLIENT!
ADDITIONAL DEATH SENTENCE...
...BY STRANGULATION!
FSHZZ—KRRBOOM

WOO HOOO!
FOR THE LAST TIME! WHERE DID YOU GET THIS MAP?
GZZT...IT... IT BELONGED TO A MAN... A FOREIGNER!
GZZT... RICHARD ALCOVA, I THINK...
HE...HE'S IN JAIL... GZZT...
RICHARD?

YOUR HONOR!

YES! WHAT WOULD YOU LIKE?

I CALL RICHARD ALDANA AS A WITNESS!

GRANTED! GUARD, BRING THE AFOREMENTIONED DETAINEE!
UM...YOU SURE?

OF COURSE I'M SURE! YOU DON'T WANT TO UPSET THE LADY, DO YOU?

GZZT...
MY VALLEY...

SIR?
GZZ...?
EHHH...
GZZ...
LISTEN, I DON'T KNOW WHAT YOU'VE BEEN TOLD ABOUT THE VALLEY OF KINGS, BUT...
...PEOPLE GET SICK AND DIE THERE TOO... NOBODY LIVES FOREVER...
THAT'S THE WAY IT IS...
BUT, YES, IT TRULY IS A BEAUTIFUL PLACE.
AND IF ONE DAY YOU COME VISIT...
...I'LL BE GLAD TO WELCOME YOU.
I CAN'T OFFER YOU ETERNAL LIFE, BUT I'M A DECENT COOK.
GLZZ...

MOM, HOW COME YOU'RE SO STRONG?
YOU CAN DO THE SCHOOL-OF-THE-HEAVENS SUMMONING. BUT ME...
ADRIAN!

CAN YOU TEACH ME?

SUMMONING? BUT YOU ALREADY KNOW HOW TO DO THEM...
NO, I DON'T. NOT LIKE YOU.

THE ONE YOU DID AT THE GRAND FINALS WAS REALLY GOOD.
NO, I MESSED IT UP.

OKAY, I PROMISE I'LL SHOW YOU.
SWEAR?
SOLEMNLY SWEAR!

CITIZENS OF NILLIPOLIS, FRIENDS OF JUSTICE—THE COURT CALLS RICHARD ALDANA TO THE WITNESS STAND!
MARIANNE, ADRIAN... I'M SORRY...
FRANCIS?

GUARD! I ASKED YOU FOR RICHARD ALDANA!
BUT, YOUR HONOR, HE WAS THE ONLY ONE IN ALDANA'S CELL!
UM...
YOU MUST'VE MADE A MISTAKE.
FRANCIS!
LISTEN, YOU SAID CELL 506-B, AND HERE HE IS!
IF YOU'RE NOT HAPPY ABOUT IT, GO COMPLAIN TO MANAGEMENT!

MARIANNE, WHAT HAPPENED? I WAS SO WORRIED...
YOU'RE NOT HURT?
I'M OKAY, BUT YOUR CRIMINAL JUSTICE SYSTEM NEEDS A FEW TWEAKS...
I THINK IT'S HIGH TIME FOR ADRIAN AND ME TO GO HOME.

OKAY, WONDERFUL! IN THE MATTER OF NILLIPOLIS VERSUS VELBA...
...I DECLARE MARIANNE VELBA GUILTY AND SENTENCE HER TO LIFE IMPRISONMENT FOR NON COMPLIANCE WITH THE FAMILY VALUES OF NILLIPOLIS, WHICH ARE THE PRIDE OF THIS GREAT CITY...
HUH?
WHAT?!
GUARDS! PLEASE SEIZE HER.

SCREW YOU, WINCHESTER!
MARIANNE WON!
JUSTICE FOR MARIANNE!
JUSTICE FOR MARIANNE!
DOWN WITH THE JUDGE!
RATA TA TA TA
GULP!
HIP!
RATA TA TA TA TA
C'MON!
LET'S GO.

AH!
WAAAH!
WAIT!
YAAAH!

EXCUSE ME!
MY PURSE...?
IF YOU DON'T MIND...

HERE!
THANKS.

MARIANNE...
YOU'LL HAVE TO EXPLAIN ALL OF THIS TO ME.
WHAT ABOUT FLORA? WE CAN'T JUST LEAVE HER!
BLAM!
OW!
WE HAVE TO GO SAVE HER!

THAT WAS THE PLAN: PICK HER UP AND THEN GO TO FRANCIS'S. OKAY?
OKAY.
JUSTICE! JUSTICE!
JUSTICE!
JUSTICE!
DOWN WITH THE BASTARDS!

TEE HEE HEE...
OH MY, WHAT A STORY...
YOU KNOW, IN ALL THE YEARS I'VE BEEN IN THIS CITY, I'VE NEVER SEEN CHAOS LIKE THAT.

MY LITTLE FRANCIS, THAT'S QUITE A CHARACTER YOU RAN INTO...
THIS MARIANNE WAS SOMETHING ELSE.
I AGREE, MR. JACOBS.

WE WEREN'T ABLE TO GET THAT MONEY BACK, BUT...
...THANKS TO HER...

...WE'VE GOT A BUNCH OF NEW REGULARS.
AND THAT JUDGE WINCHESTER SCUMBAG WON'T BE SHOWING UP.
BEEP-BEEP!

NOT TO MENTION I'D STILL BE ROTTING IN JAIL IF IT WEREN'T FOR HER.
OH NO, I WAS THERE!
YOU'RE SWEET!

I WONDERED WHY YOU WERE SO SMITTEN WITH THAT GIRL.
WHO, MARIANNE?
AND THEN I REMEMBERED...

THAT PICTURE OF MERILYN IN YOUR ROOM...
SHE KIND OF LOOKS LIKE HER.

WHEN I TOOK THEM TO THE BOAT THIS MORNING, ADRIAN GAVE ME A MESSAGE FOR YOU...

HE SAID, "TELL FLORA I'M GOING TO MISS HER A LOT."
AW... THAT BOY'S ADORABLE.

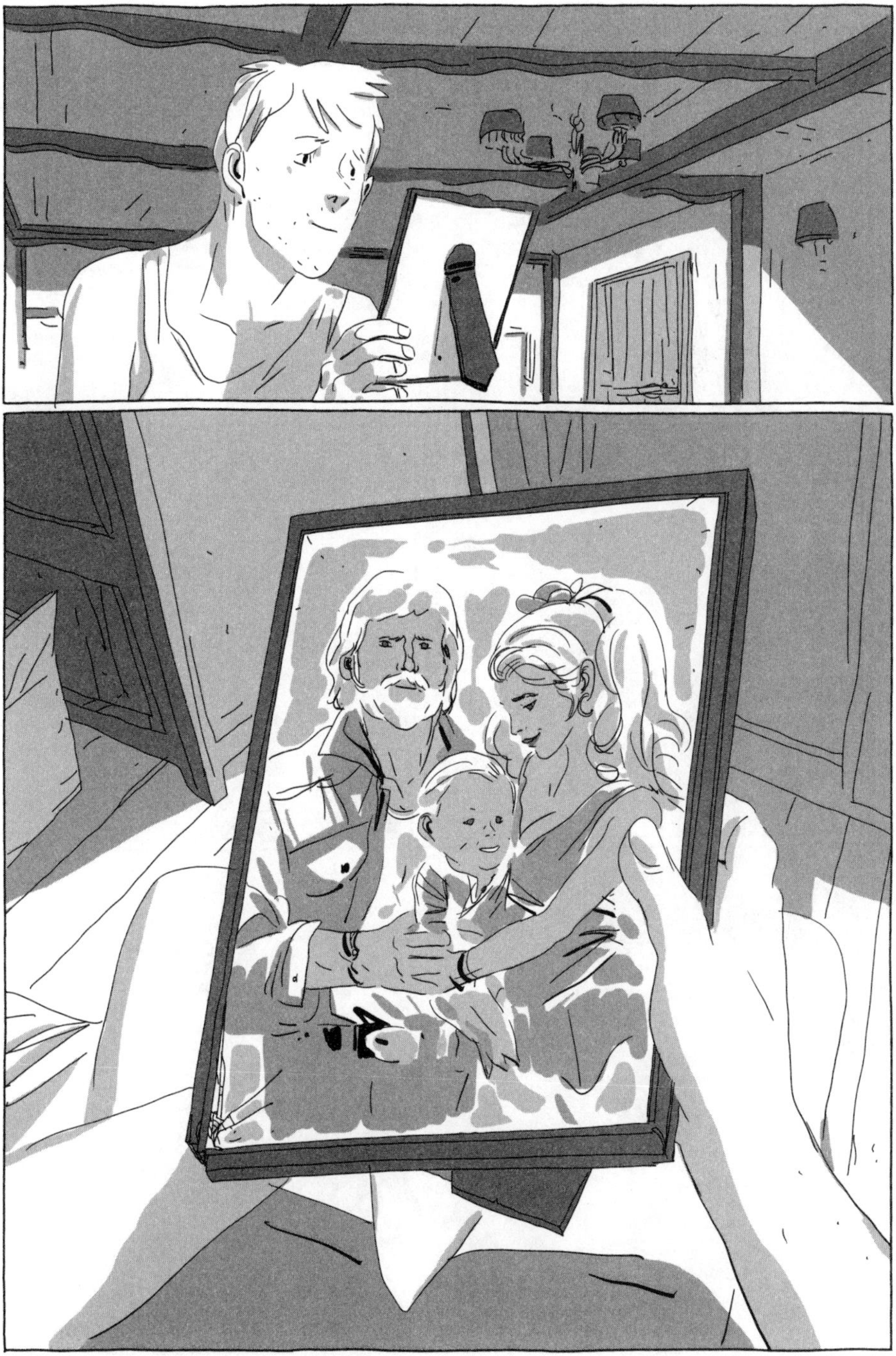

FRANCIS?
SORRY TO BOTHER YOU SO EARLY, BUT WE'RE HEADING OFF.
NO, IT'S FINE!
YOU'RE GOING BACK TO THE VALLEY?
LET ME THROW SOME CLOTHES ON AND–
OH! I HAVE SOMETHING TO SHOW YOU.

WELL...
SORRY, MY STUFF'S A BIT OF A MESS...
AH, HERE!

IT'S TOO BAD YOU NEVER MENTIONED THE NAME OF THE MAN YOU WERE LOOKING FOR...
RICHARD ALDANA.

BAWWW
ROCCAFORTE

WHOOOOAAA

PAXTOWN?
I'M ALMOST CERTAIN THAT'S WHERE THE GUY WHO KNOCKED ME OUT WAS FROM.
AND HE MUST'VE TAKEN RICHARD ALDANA BACK WITH HIM.

THE TANKER'S CAPTAIN IS AN OLD FRIEND OF MY DAD'S. IN A FEW HOURS YOU'LL BE OFF THE ISLAND.
ISLAND?

NILLIPOLIS. ONCE YOU REACH THE CONTINENT...
...YOU SHOULDN'T HAVE ANY TROUBLE FINDING RICHARD.

BUT WATCH OUT. PAXTOWN MAY BE MORE UPSCALE THAN THIS, BUT IT'S STILL PRETTY ROUGH.
GO TO THIS ADDRESS AND ASK FOR FIONA MERY.
I'VE SENT WORD YOU'RE COMING.

THANKS, FRANCIS.

WE DON'T SEE EACH OTHER MUCH, WHAT WITH THE DISTANCE AND ALL...
...BUT I KNOW SHE'LL DO WHATEVER SHE CAN TO HELP.

YOU'VE DONE A LOT FOR US.
NO, MARIANNE, YOU'VE DONE A LOT FOR ME. IT'S BEEN A PLEASURE KNOWING YOU.

LOOK AFTER YOURSELVES OVER THERE. PROMISE?

PROMISE.
PROMISE.

BAAAWWWWW
WWWWW
NILLIPOLIS TANKER

BYE, ADRIAN!
GOOD-BYE, FRANCIS!

AND TELL FLORA I'M GONNA MISS HER A LOT!

FLORA? REALLY? I DIDN'T REALIZE...
SHE WAS NICE TO ME.
WHAT ABOUT YOUR GIRLFRIEND ELORNA?
THAT'S DIFFERENT.

I'M SORRY, ADRIAN.
WHAT FOR?

...DO YOU WANT US TO GO HOME?
JUST SAY THE WORD, AND WE'LL GO BACK.

ADRIAN...

I'VE GOT SOME SCORES TO SETTLE, AND YOU, POOR THING, GOT CAUGHT IN THE MIDDLE.
JUST TELL ME WHAT YOU WANT. IF YOU WANT TO HEAD BACK, WE'LL DO IT.

NAH. I WANNA GO FARTHER.
THOUGH I DO GET MAD SOMETIMES WHEN YOU YELL AT ME.

YOU DON'T MISS THE VALLEY?

I MISS ONI A BIT...
...BUT IT'S MORE FUN OVER HERE!

YOU KNOW, YOUR MOM'S REAL LUCKY TO HAVE A SON LIKE YOU.

CAST OFF!
OFF WE GO!

PACK OF LOAFING RATS! WHAT THE...
GET YER MAGGOTY ASSES BACK DOWN TO THE MACHINE ROOM!

WE'RE GOOD, CAPTAIN. PABLO'S GOT THINGS UNDER CONTROL DOWN THERE...
ARE YOU OUT OF YOUR MIND? IS PABLO ON LOOKOUT TOO, AND IN THE WEAPONS ROOM, AND ON THE FRONT DECK? HAS HE GOT THAT UNDER CONTROL TOO?

IF PIRATES ATTACK, YOU'LL BE THE FIRST ONES GETTING THEIR THROATS SLIT!!!

NO OFFENSE, CAPTAIN, BUT THERE AREN'T ANY PIRATES LEFT. WE WERE THE LAST ONES...

GET BACK TO YOUR STATIONS! ALL OF YOU! AND WHAT ARE THOSE CIVILIANS DOING ON DECK? THEY SHOULD BE IN THEIR CABIN!
SINCE YOU SMACKED AROUND THAT JUDGE WINCHESTER PIECE OF TRASH, YOU'VE EARNED MY ETERNAL GRATITUDE...
THAT VERMIN IS 100% PURE PAXTOWN. THE CITY'S A CESSPOOL.

IF ANYTHING GOES WRONG WHEN YOU GET THERE, THE ROCCAFORTE WILL BE DOCKED ALL DAY.
THANK YOU, SIR.

ALL RIGHT, MOVE IT! I WANT TO SEE PAXTOWN BEFORE NOON!

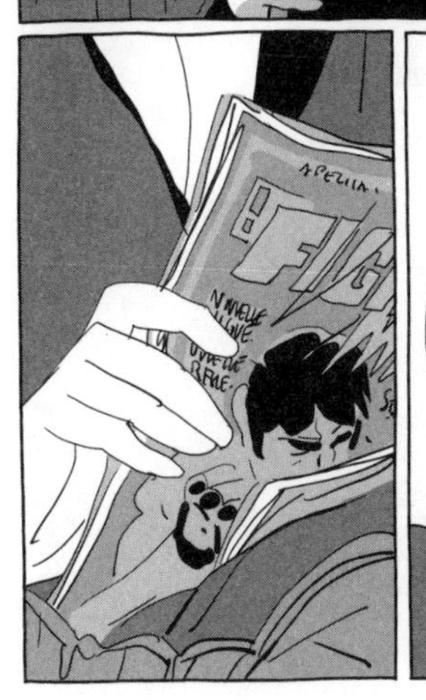

SCANDAL!
Final match ends in shame: Aldana banned from league for life!
WHO ARE YOU, RICHARD ALDANA?

CAW
CAW
CAW
CAW
CAW
CAW
HEY, LOSER! WAKE UP!

GET UP, ALDANA!
HMM?
ASSWIPE! GET UP!
YOU STINK!
TAP!
BREAKFAST IS SERVED.
HEY!
BLAM!
JONIO?
UGH!

WHO THE HELL ARE YOU?
ROOM SERVICE...?
AND WHERE ARE WE?
LET HIM GO, ALDANA!
NOW, GODDAMN IT!
YOU DON'T STAND A CHANCE!

DROP IT AND PUT YOUR HANDS BEHIND YOUR HEAD!
OKAY!
GRAB HIM!
HEY!
I WARNED THEM YOU WERE GRUMPY IN THE MORNING!
MR. H?
RELEASE HIM!

SHKRR!

HOW LONG WERE YOU FOLLOWING ME?
OH, YOU KNOW...
SLAP!

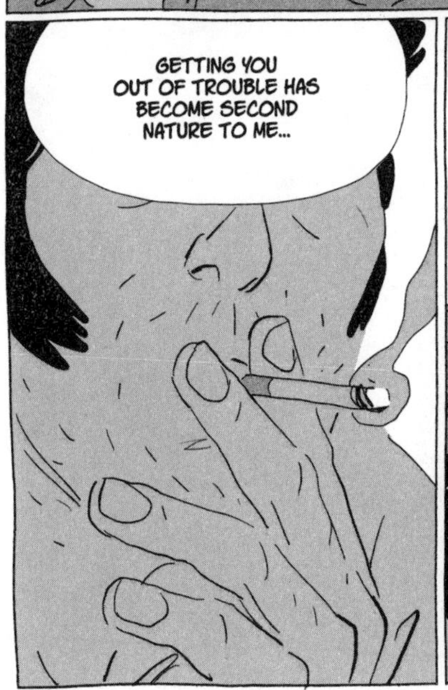
GETTING YOU OUT OF TROUBLE HAS BECOME SECOND NATURE TO ME...

I KNOW WHY YOU'RE HERE, H...!
LISTEN, I'VE GOT THE MONEY. IT'S IN MY BAG IN NILLIPOLIS. IF WE JUST TURN AROUND AND–

FORGET THE MONEY! MILO WROTE IT OFF AGES AGO!
IT'S YOUR SKINNY ASS HE WANTS TO SEE.

I'M GUESSING YOU CAN'T JUST TELL HIM YOU DIDN'T FIND ME?

SORRY, RICHARD.

YOU WANT
US TO CUFF HIM,
BOSS?
NO NEED!
HE'S GOT
NOWHERE
TO GO.
I CAN'T
BELIEVE IT!
I WOULD'VE CHUCKED
HIM INTO THE WATER
ONCE AND FOR ALL.
YOU'RE
COLD,
BOBBY.
IT'S THE
LEAST HE
DESERVES!
IF I'D BEEN THE
REFEREE, I WOULDA
PUT A BULLET IN
HIS BRAIN!
I THINK
HE PAID FOR WHAT
HE DID!
PAID, MY ASS!
AND WHAT ABOUT
THE CITY'S HONOR?
WHO CAN PAY FOR
THAT?

PAXTOWN'S HONOR? ARE YOU KIDDING?
EVERYONE'S BEEN WIPING THEIR ASSES WITH IT SINCE FOREVER!

CRRR...
WE'RE DOCKING IN FIVE MINUTES...
ALL HANDS ON DECK!
THERE SHE IS!
PAXTOWN'S AN INTERESTING PLACE...
QUITE A JUMP FROM THE VALLEY OF KINGS, I IMAGINE.

BUT SOMETHING TELLS ME YOU'RE GOING TO LIKE IT.

Read on for a preview of

4

The Show

Balak + Sanlaville + Vivès

Available in February 2016 by First Second Books

ISBN 978-1-62672-049-7

HA HA HA... YOU WERE PARTNERS? IS THAT SO, RICHARD?

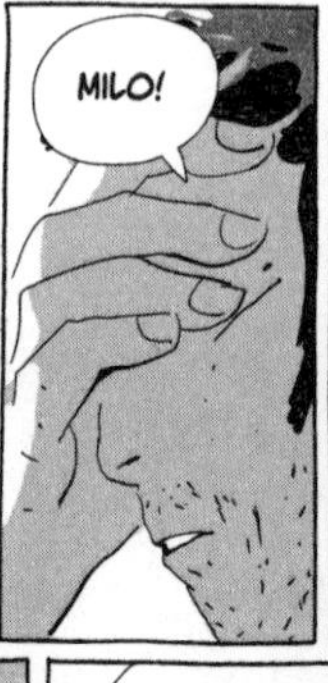
MILO!

WHAT'S YOUR NAME, KID?
ADRIAN VELBA.

ADRIAN VELBA! THAT'S A PERFECT CHAMP'S NAME! DID YOU KNOW WE HAD AN ADRIAN WHO WON THE FFFC HERE? SOME 20 YEARS AGO.
WHAT'S THE FFFC?
THE FIGHTING FISTS FUNERAL CUP. IT'S THE TOURNAMENT I RUN.

RICHARD! YOU HEAR? THEY HAVE A TOURNAMENT HERE! LET'S PARTNER UP!
ADRIAN...

YEAH, RICHARD, THAT'S A GREAT IDEA!
YOU WERE JUST LOOKING FOR A PARTNER, WEREN'T YOU?

CUT THE CRAP, MILO.
IT'S NOT A GAME. LEAVE THE KID OUT OF IT.

COME ON, RICHARD, YOU GUYS WON THE ROYAL FLUSH OR SOMETHING...
YOU GUYS MAKE A GREAT TEAM, RIGHT?
MILO, YOU BASTARD...
STOP IT!
YOU KNOW WHAT, ADRIAN? I'M GONNA SIGN YOU UP WITH RICHARD. IT'LL BE—
MILO!
I TOLD YOU TO LEAVE HIM OUT OF IT!
HE'S JUST A KID—HE CAN'T FIGHT. IT'S A JOKE!
I'M YOUR PROBLEM, NOT HIM!
YOU...
?

WHY ARE YOU SAYING THAT...
...I DON'T KNOW HOW TO FIGHT?

ADRIAN, IT'S FOR YOUR OWN-
THAT'S ENOUGH!

MY SON ISN'T GOOD ENOUGH FOR THE GREAT RICHARD ALDANA?

YOU DON'T NEED HIM ANYMORE...
SO YOU JUST DUMP HIM?

MARIANNE, FOR GOD'S SAKE!
THIS ISN'T THE TIME FOR THAT!

REMEMBER WHAT I TOLD YOU IN THE VALLEY, RICHARD?
IF YOU HURT ADRIAN...

...THERE WON'T BE A PLACE IN THE WORLD WHERE YOU CAN HIDE.

MR. ZOTIS, IS IT?
HMM?
YOU'RE GOING TO SIGN UP MY SON AND ME IN YOUR TOURNAMENT.

...
REALLY?
HMM...

New York

Published by First Second
First Second is an imprint of Roaring Brook Press,
a division of Holtzbrinck Publishing Holdings Limited Partnership
175 Fifth Avenue, New York, New York 10010

Library of Congress Control Number: 2015937859

ISBN: 978-1-62672-048-0

First Second books may be purchased for business or promotional use. For information on bulk purchases please contact Macmillan Corporate and Premium Sales Department at (800) 221-7945 x5442 or by email at specialmarkets@macmillan.com.

Originally published in France by Casterman as *Lastman tome 3*.

First American edition 2015

Cover design by Danielle Ceccolini
Book design by Rob Steen

Printed in the United States of America

10 9 8 7 6 5 4 3 2 1